Inside Out

Upper Intermediate Companion

German Edition

Sue Kay & Vaughan Jones

MACMILLAN

CONTENTS

WORDLIST

Welcome to the *Inside Out* Upper Intermediate Companion!

What information does the *Inside Out* Upper Intermediate Companion give you?
- a summary of key words and phrases from each unit of *Inside Out* Upper Intermediate Student's Book
- pronunciation of the key words and phrases
- translations of the key words and phrases
- sample sentences showing the words and phrases in context
- a summary of the Grammar Reference from *Inside Out* Upper Intermediate Student's Book

Abbreviations used in the Companion

(art)	article	(phr v)	phrasal verb	(m)	masculine	(Am E)	American English
(v)	verb	(pron)	pronoun	(pl n)	plural noun		
(v*)	irregular verb	(prep)	preposition	(adv)	adverb	(TS)	Tapescript
(adj)	adjective	(det)	determiner	(conj)	conjunction		
(n)	noun	(f)	feminine				

VOWELS AND DIPHTHONGS

/ɪ/	big fish	/bɪg fɪʃ/	/ɑː/	calm start	/kɑːm stɑːt/
/iː/	green beans	/griːn biːnz/	/ɒ/	hot spot	/hɒt spɒt/
/ʊ/	should look	/ʃʊd lʊk/	/ɪə/	ear	/ɪə/
/uː/	blue moon	/bluː muːn/	/eɪ/	face	/feɪs/
/e/	ten eggs	/ten egz/	/ʊə/	pure	/pjʊə(r)/
/ə/	about mother	/əbaʊt mʌðə/	/ɔɪ/	boy	/bɔɪ/
/ɜː/	learn words	/lɜːn wɜːdz/	/əʊ/	nose	/nəʊz/
/ɔː/	short talk	/ʃɔːt tɔːk/	/eə/	hair	/heə/
/æ/	fat cat	/fæt kæt/	/aɪ/	eye	/aɪ/
/ʌ/	must come	/mʌst kʌm/	/aʊ/	mouth	/maʊθ/

CONSONANTS

/p/	pen	/pen/	/s/	snake	/sneɪk/
/b/	bad	/bæd/	/z/	noise	/nɔɪz/
/t/	tea	/tiː/	/ʃ/	shop	/ʃɒp/
/d/	dog	/dɒg/	/ʒ/	measure	/meʒə(r)/
/tʃ/	church	/tʃɜːtʃ/	/m/	make	/meɪk/
/dʒ/	jazz	/dʒæz/	/n/	nine	/naɪn/
/k/	cost	/kɒst/	/ŋ/	sing	/sɪŋ/
/g/	girl	/gɜːl/	/h/	house	/haʊs/
/f/	far	/fɑː(r)/	/l/	leg	/leg/
/v/	voice	/vɔɪs/	/r/	red	/red/
/θ/	thin	/θɪn/	/w/	wet	/wet/
/ð/	then	/ðen/	/j/	yes	/jes/

Unit 1

Images/Close up (p. 4–5)

momentous (adj)	/məˈmentəs/	denkwürdig	Seeing a man on the moon was a **momentous** event.
bitterness (n) (TS)	/ˈbɪtənəs/	Verbitterung	He appeared to feel no anger or **bitterness**.
kid (n)	/kɪd/	Kind	When I was a **kid** I always hoped to see a man on the moon.
newsflash (n)	/ˈnjuːzflæʃ/	Nachrichten	I remember seeing a **newsflash** on TV.
way of life (n)	/ˌweɪ əv ˈlaɪf/	Lebensart	Punk wasn't just a fashion – it was a **way of life**.
annoy (v)	/əˈnɔɪ/	ärgern	It **annoys** me when people say punk was just a fashion.
in spite of	/ɪn ˈspaɪt əv/	trotz	**In spite of** everything he showed no bitterness.
lose touch with	/luːz ˈtʌtʃ wɪð/	den Kontakt verlieren	I don't want to **lose touch with** my friends.

Auxiliary verbs/So & neither/Question tags (p. 6–7)

spoiled (adj)	/spɔɪld/	verwöhnt	Were you **spoiled** as a child?
weird (adj)	/wɪəd/	merkwürdig	'I went to Rosefield High school.' 'That's **weird**, so did I!'
fluently (adv)	/ˈfluːəntlɪ/	fließend	He speaks English **fluently**.
sure (adv)	/ʃʊə(r)/	sicher	'Do you remember Mrs Rivers?' 'The math teacher? **Sure**.'
nap (n)	/næp/	Nickerchen	If you feel tired, go and have a **nap**.
vacation (n) (Am E) (TS)	/vəˈkeɪʃn/verˈkeɪʃn/	Ferien, Urlaub	We're on **vacation** in London.
Go ahead. (phr v) (TS)	/ˌgəʊ əˈhed/	Nur zu.	'Is it okay if I sit here?' '**Go ahead.**'
revise (v)	/rɪˈvaɪz/	wiederholen	I've got to **revise** for my exam.
to be honest (TS)	/tə biː ˈɒnɪst/	um ehrlich zu sein	**To be honest**, I don't like London.
You're kidding! (TS)	/jʊə(r) ˈkɪdɪŋ/	Kaum zu glauben.	'I'm from Santa Barbara.' '**You're kidding** – so am I!'

Image queen (p. 9–10)

burning (adj)	/ˈbɜːnɪŋ/	glühend	She had a **burning** ambition to become famous.
calculating (adj)	/ˌkælkjəˈleɪtɪŋ/	berechnend	I don't like people who are **calculating**.
complex (adj)	/ˈkɒmpleks/	vielseitig	Madonna is a **complex** and clever woman.
feisty (adj)	/ˈfaɪstɪ/	lebhaft	Women nowadays are more **feisty** and independent.
glitzy (adj)	/ˈglɪtsɪ/	funkelnd	Do you like wearing **glitzy** jewellery?
glossy (adj)	/ˈglɒsɪ/	glänzend	At that time she had dark **glossy** hair.
joint (adj)	/dʒɔɪnt/	gemeinsam	They were involved in a **joint** film venture.
menacing (adj)	/ˈmenəsɪŋ/	drohend	Some of her outfits looked **menacing**.

notorious (adj)	/nəʊˈtɔːrɪəs/	berüchtigt	The geisha is one of the most **notorious** symbols of pre-feminist women.
scheming (adj)	/ˈskiːmɪŋ/	raffiniert	**Scheming** people will do anything to get what they want.
space-age (adj)	/ˈspeɪseɪdʒ/	futuristisch	What do you think of her **space-age** costumes?
stark (adj)	/stɑːk/	schlechthin	It is the **stark** image of a geisha.
submissive (adj)	/səbˈmɪsɪv/	unterwürfig	Geisha girls were silent and **submissive**.
thought-out (adj)	/θɔːtˈaʊt/	durchdacht	Every change of image is a carefully **thought-out** strategy.
torn (adj)	/tɔːn/	zerrissen	Your tights are **torn**!
trashy (adj)	/ˈtræʃɪ/	kitschig	She first appeared as a **trashy** punk.
uncanny (adj)	/ʌnˈkænɪ/	unheimlich	There's an **uncanny** resemblance between her and her mother.
achievement (n)	/əˈtʃiːvmənt/	Leistung	Modelling make-up at the age of 40 is quite an **achievement**!
adaptation (n)	/ædæpˈteɪʃn/	(Film-)Bearbeitung	Spielberg is doing a film **adaptation** of Memoirs of a Geisha.
bob (n)	/bɒb/	Bubikopf	Have you always worn your hear in a **bob**?
bra top (n)	/ˈbrɑː tɒp/	Oberteil (Bikini/Top)	She used to wear conical **bra top**s.
charts (n)	/tʃɑːts/	Hitliste	Holiday was in the **charts** in 1984.
consolidator (n)	/kənˈsɒlɪdeɪtə(r)/	Trendfolger	She's a **consolidator** of trends.
convent girl (n)	/ˈkɒnvənt ˌɡɜːl/	Nonne	Madonna was a **convent girl** in Detroit.
corset (n)	/ˈkɔːsɪt/	Mieder	She used to wear tight **corset**s.
decade (n)	/ˈdekeɪd/	Jahrzehnt	She's one of the most famous stars of the past two **decade**s.
Earth Mother (n)	/ˈɜːθ ˌmʌðə(r)/	Urmutter	After the birth of her daughter she became an **Earth Mother**.
era (n)	/ˈɪərə/	Zeitalter	We're living in the post-feminist **era**.
furs (n)	/fɜːz/	Pelz	Many people now disapprove of wearing **furs**.
gash (n)	/ɡæʃ/	tiefe Wunde	Her red lips looked like a **gash** on her face.
look (n)	/lʊk/	Aussehen	Do you like Madonna's latest **look**?
real life (n)	/ˌrɪəl ˈlaɪf/	das wirkliche Leben	Have you ever seen a famous person in **real life**?
reinvention (n)	/ˌriːɪnˈvenʃn/	Kreieren eines neuen Images	Madonna is a mistress of **reinvention**.
resemblance (n)	/rɪˈzembləns/	Ähnlichkeit	There was a strong **resemblance** between her and Eva Peron.
subservience (n)	/səbˈsɜːvɪəns/	Dienstbereitschaft	Geishas were known for their **subservience**.
tights (n)	/taɪts/	Strumpfhose	She appeared as a punk with torn **tights**.
transformation (n)	/ˌtrænsfəˈmeɪʃn/	Umwandlung	I couldn't believe how different she looked. What a **transformation**!
venture (n)	/ˈventʃə(r)/	Unternehmen	Beatty and Madonna were involved in a joint film **venture**.
bounce into (phr v)	/ˈbaʊns ˌɪntə/	den Sprung schaffen in	She first **bounced into** the charts in 1984.
emerge as (phr v)	/ɪˈmɜːdʒ ˌəz/	erscheinen als	When her daughter was nine months old, she **emerged as** an Earth Mother.
move on (phr v)	/ˌmuːv ˈɒn/	sich vorwärtsbewegen	Sometimes you just have to **move on** in life.
pay off (phr v)	/ˌpeɪ ˈɒf/	zu einem Ergebnis führen	All our hard work finally **paid off**.
pick up on (phr v)	/ˌpɪk ˈʌp ɒn/	aufnehmen	She **picked up on** the look and made it her own.
stare into (phr v)	/ˈsteər ˌɪntə(r)/	starren in	She stood **staring into** the camera.
sum up (phr v)	/ˌsʌm ˈʌp/	zusammenfassen	Madonna's life **sums up** female independence.

2

turn to (phr v)	/ˈtɜːn ˌtə/	sich wenden an	She **turned to** Jean-Paul Gaultier for a new look.
adopt (v)	/əˈdɒpt/	sich zulegen	Do you enjoy **adopting** new looks?
blame (v)	/bleɪm/	etwas übel nehmen	You can't **blame** her for her decision.
draw (v)	/drɔː/	anziehen	What has **drawn** her to the geisha image?
entrance (v)	/ɪnˈtrɑːns/	entzücken	Sean Penn was **entranced** by her image.
frame (v)	/freɪm/	umrahmen	Her white face was **framed** by long dark hair.
hitch-hike (v)	/ˈhɪtʃhaɪk/	trampen	It can be dangerous to **hitch-hike**.
imprison (v)	/ɪmˈprɪzn/	einsperren	Geishas were **imprisoned** in the service of men.
secure (v)	/sɪˈkjʊə(r)/	sich etwas sichern	She was keen to **secure** the part in Spielberg's movie.
be involved with	/ˌbiː ɪnˈvɒlvd wɪð/	ein Verhältnis haben mit	She **was involved with** Warren Beatty for a time.
be the mistress of	/ˌbɪ ðə ˈmɪstrəs əv/	Meisterin sein im	She **is the mistress of** reinvention.
become aware of	/bɪˌkʌm əˈweə(r) əv/	aufmerksam werden auf	I first **became aware of** Kylie Minogue back in 1988.
dead straight	/ˌded ˈstreɪt/	völlig glatt	She wears her hair **dead straight**.
down to the last detail	/ˌdaʊn tə ðə ˌlɑːst ˈdiːteɪl/	bis ins kleinste Detail	The image is always perfect – **down to the last detail**.
have one's eye on	/ˌhæv wʌnz ˈaɪ ɒn/	ein Auge auf etwas werfen	Do you **have your eye on** a part in another film?
make sth one's own	/ˌmeɪk sʌmθɪŋ wʌnz ˈəʊn/	sich etwas aneignen	She's **made each look her own**.
take sb at face value	/ˌteɪk sʌmbədɪ ət ˌfeɪs ˈvæljuː/	sich vom ersten Eindruck leiten lassen	It would be a mistake to **take her at face value**.
take sth seriously	/ˌteɪk ðɪs ˈsɪərɪəslɪ/	etwas ernst nehmen	She **takes all her roles seriously**.
Time will tell.	/ˌtaɪm wɪl ˈtel/	Das wird sich zeigen.	"Will she get the part in the film?" "**Time will tell.**"
every	/ˈevrɪ/	jede(r)	Her hair has been **every** colour under the sun.
vanish from view	/ˌvænɪʃ frəm ˈvjuː/	außer Sichtweite geraten	During the pregnancy she **vanished from view**.

You are what you wear (p. 11–12)

neat (adj) (TS)	/niːt/	ordentlich	His clothes are always clean and **neat**.
smart (adj) (TS)	/smɑːt/	schick	Charles always looks **smart**.
feature (n) (TS)	/ˈfiːtʃə(r)/	Leitartikel	I'm doing a **feature** on men's clothing.
item of clothing (n)	/ˌaɪtəm əv ˈkləʊðɪŋ/	Kleidungsstück	What's your favourite **item of clothing**?
lookalike (n) (Am E)	/ˈlʊkəlaɪk/	Doppelgänger	Beckham got tired of all the **lookalike**s.
research (n) (TS)	/rɪˈsɜːtʃ ˈriːsɜːtʃ/	Forschung	I'm doing some **research** for an article.
self-esteem (n) (TS)	/ˌself ɪˈstiːm/	Selbstachtung	He has good **self-esteem**.
self-image (n)	/ˌself ˈɪmɪdʒ/	Selbstbild	What do your clothes say about your **self-image**?
survey (n) (TS)	/ˈsɜːveɪ/	Untersuchung	Would you mind helping me with a **survey**?
tattoo (n)	/təˈtuː/	Tätowierung	Does David Beckham have any **tattoo**s?
dress up (phr v) (TS)	/ˌdres ˈʌp/	sich herausputzen	Do you like **dressing up**?
shave (v)	/ʃeɪv/	rasieren	Why did he **shave** his head?
couldn't live without	/ˌkʊdnt ˌlɪv wɪˈðaʊt/	nicht ohne etw. leben können	Matt **couldn't live without** his trainers.

feel tempted (Am E)	/ˌfiːl ˈtemptəd/	in Versuchung geraten	I sometimes **feel tempted** to change my image.
get fed up (with) (Am E)	/ˌget fed ˈʌp (wɪð)/	etwas satt bekommen	He **got fed up** with all the lookalikes.
go clubbing (TS)	/ɡəʊ ˈklʌbɪŋ/	Nachtlokale besuchen	Do you dress up to **go clubbing?**
put it this way (TS)	/ˌpʊt ɪt ˈðɪs weɪ/	sagen wir so	Well, **put it this way** – I don't wear a suit.

Unit 2

Family/Problem Parents (p. 14–15)

all-in-one (adj)	/ˌɔːlɪnˈwʌn/	einteilig	To imitate Cher she wears an **all-in-one** body stocking.
amused (by) (adj)	/əˈmjuːzd (baɪ)/	amüsiert (über)	The crowd was **amused** by the sight of Kayleigh and her mum.
annoyed (with) (adj)	/əˈnɔɪd (wɪð)/	verärgert (über)	Why are you **annoyed** with me?
dull (adj)	/dʌl/	langweilig	Life's never **dull** with Mum around!
gorgeous (adj)	/ˈɡɔːdʒəs/	prächtig, bezaubernd	Gina admits that her mum is **gorgeous**.
humiliated (by) (adj)	/hjuːˈmɪlieɪtəd (baɪ)/	gedemütigt (durch)	Alex felt **humiliated** by his dad's behaviour.
irritated (with) (adj)	/ˈɪrɪteɪtəd (wɪð)/	verärgert (über)	Teenagers often feel **irritated** with their parents.
loud (adj)	/laʊd/	laut	Alex's dad is a **loud** person.
outrageous (adj)	/aʊtˈreɪdʒəs/	ausgefallen	Cher is known for her **outrageous** clothes.
proud (of)	/praʊd (əv)/	stolz (auf)	Congratulations! We're really **proud** of you.
see-through (adj)	/ˈsiːθruː/	durchsichtig	Gina's mum wears a black **see-through** body stocking.
eventually (adv)	/ɪˈventʃʊəlɪ/	schließlich	**Eventually** Alex's friends found out that his dad was a clown.
act (n)	/ækt/	Nummer	People often stare at Gina while her mum does her **act**.
ball girl (n)	/ˈbɔːl ˌɡɜːl/	Ballmädchen	Kayleigh is a **ball girl** at the football ground.
cosmetic surgery (n)	/kɒzˌmetɪk ˈsɜːdʒərɪ/	plastische Chirurgie	She manages to stay young without **cosmetic surgery**.
embarrassment (n)	/ɪmˈbærəsmənt/	Peinlichkeit	Mum causes us a lot of **embarrassment**.
ground (n)	/ɡraʊnd/	Gelände	Sometimes mum chases me round the **ground**!
humiliation (n)	/hjuːˌmɪliˈeɪʃn/	Erniedrigung	I couldn't stand the **humiliation** of seeing my dad dressed up as a clown!
lace (n)	/leɪs/	Spitze	She wears a body stocking made of **lace**.
limelight (n)	/ˈlaɪmlaɪt/	Rampenlicht	Do you like being in the **limelight**?
mascot (n)	/ˈmæskɒt/	Maskottchen	She's the club **mascot** and wears a bird costume.
nightmare (n)	/ˈnaɪtmeə(r)/	Alptraum	It's a **nightmare** if I'm at a club when Mum's performing!
clown around (phr v)	/ˌklaʊn əˈraʊnd/	den Clown spielen	Stop **clowning around**!
find out (phr v)	/ˌfaɪnd ˈvaʊt/	etwas herausbekommen	My friends eventually **found out** that Dad was a clown.
fool around (phr v)	/ˌfuːl əˈraʊnd/	sich närrisch benehmen	She has to **fool around** to entertain the crowd.
hear about (phr v)	/ˈhɪə(r) əbaʊt/	von etwas Wind bekommen	I don't know what will happen when my friends **hear about** it.
join in (phr v)	/ˌdʒɔɪn ˈɪn/	mitmachen	Dad used to make me **join in** his act.

open up (phr v)	/ˌəʊpən ˈʌp/	sich öffnen	I was so embarrassed – I just wanted the ground to **open up**!
run away (phr v)	/ˌrʌn əˈweɪ/	wegrennen	When Kayleigh **runs away** her mum tries to catch her.
chase (v)	/tʃeɪs/	verfolgen	Mum loves **chasing** me round the ground.
compensate (v)	/ˈkɒmpenseɪt/	ausgleichen	Dad paid me but nothing could **compensate** for the humiliation.
cuddle (v)	/ˈkʌdl/	liebkosen	She makes me **cuddle** her in front of the whole crowd!
dread (v)	/dred/	fürchten	Alex **dreaded** his friends finding out that his dad was a clown.
entertain (v)	/ˌentəˈteɪn/	unterhalten	A club mascot has to **entertain** the crowd.
nickname (v)	/ˈnɪkneɪm/	einen Spitznamen geben	At first they **nicknamed** me Corky Junior.
swallow (v)	/ˈswɒləʊ/	verschlingen	I just wanted the ground to open up and **swallow** me!
whistle (v)	/ˈwɪsl/	pfeifen	Dad's always **whistling**!
round here	/ˌraʊnd ˈhɪə(r)/	in der Nähe	Everyone **round here** knows my mum as Cher.
see the funny side (of sth)	/ˌsiː ðə ˈfʌnɪ saɪd (əv sʌmθɪŋ)/	das Lustige davon sehen	Alex finds it hard to see **the funny side of** his father's **job**.
shake sb's hand	/ˌʃeɪk sʌmbɒdɪz ˈhænd/	jmd. die Hand schütteln	She went over to my Maths teacher and **shook his hand**.

Close up (p. 16–18)

reserved (adj)	/rɪˈzɜːvd/	zurückhaltend	Do you think it's true that English people are very **reserved**?
apparently (adv)	/əˈpærəntlɪ/	offensichtlich	English people don't like hugging or kissing, **apparently**.
wherever (adv)	/weə(r)ˈevə(r)/	überall wo	Home is **wherever** your friends and family are.
hug (n)	/hʌg/	Umarmung	Give me a **hug**!
loved-ones (n pl)	/ˈlʌvdwʌnz/	die Lieben	I miss my friends and **loved-ones**.
look forward to (phr v)	/ˌlʊk ˈfɔːwəd tə/	sich freuen auf	Are you **looking forward to** the holidays?
afford (v)	/əˈfɔːd/	sich etwas erlauben	I can't **afford** to go on holiday this year.
aim (v)	/eɪm/	anstreben	We **aim** to finish the work by the end of October.
allow (v)	/əˈlaʊ/	erlauben	Would you **allow** your children to stay out late?
approve (v)	/əˈpruːv/	zustimmen, für etwas sein	I don't **approve** of smoking.
arrange (v)	/əˈreɪndʒ/	verabreden	They've **arranged** to go away next weekend.
attempt (v)	/əˈtempt/	versuchen	She **attempted** to swim the English Channel.
encourage (v)	/ɪnˈkʌrɪdʒ/	ermutigen	We've always **encouraged** our kids to work hard at school.
expect (v)	/ɪkˈspekt/	erwarten	My parents **expect** me to go to university.
insist (v)	/ɪnˈsɪst/	bestehen auf	They prefer not talking about anything personal and **insist** on talking about the weather.
iron (v)	/ˈaɪən/	bügeln	I don't waste time **ironing** my clothes.
object (v)	/əbˈdʒekt/	Einspruch erheben	They **object** to talking about personal things.
remind (v)	/rɪˈmaɪnd/	jmd. erinnern	**Remind** me to go to the bank.
succeed (v)	/səkˈsiːd/	erfolgreich sein	Eva's family **succeeded** in making her feel welcome.
urge (v)	/ɜːdʒ/	dringend bitten	They **urged** her not to go out alone at night.
do sb a favour	/ˌduː sʌmbɒdɪ ə ˈfeɪvə(r)/	jmd. einen Gefallen tun	**Do me a favour** and post this letter for me.

do well	/ˌduː ˈwel/	gut sein	She's **doing** really **well** at school.
feel at home	/ˌfiːl ət ˈhəʊm/	sich wie zuhause fühlen	Eva's family made her **feel at home**.
get in the way	/ˌget ɪn ðə ˈweɪ/	im Weg sein	When I'm out with Dave and his girlfriend I always feel as if I'm **getting in the way**.
get used to	/ˌget ˈjuːst tə/	sich an etwas gewöhnen	When you live in a foreign country there are a lot of new things to **get used to**.
in return	/ˌɪn rɪˈtɜːn/	im Gegenzug	If someone does you a favour you should be willing to do them a favour **in return**.
keep sth tidy	/ˌkiːp sʌmθɪŋ ˈtaɪdɪ/	etwas ordentlich halten	Try to **keep your room tidy**.
respect one's elders	/rɪˌspekt wʌnz ˈeldəz/	seine Eltern respektieren	A lot of young people nowadays don't seem to **respect their elders**.

Meeting the parents/Close up (p. 19–21)

be allergic to (adj)	/biː əˈlɜːdʒɪk tə/	allergisch sein gegen	**I'm allergic to** cats.
compatible (adj)	/kəmˈpætəbl/	zueinander passend	Do you think Sarah and Andy are **compatible**?
essential (adj)	/ɪˈsenʃl/	wesentlich	It's not **essential** for a couple to come from the same background.
hopeless (adj)	/ˈhəʊpləs/	hoffnungslos schlecht	I'm **hopeless** at Maths.
wealthy (adj)	/ˈwelθɪ/	wohlhabend	He comes from a **wealthy** family.
anyway (adv) (TS)	/ˈenɪweɪ/	wie auch immer	**Anyway**, we don't take Sarah's relationships too seriously.
straightaway (adv) (TS)	/ˌstreɪtəˈweɪ/	auf Anhieb	Andy finds it difficult to get on with people **straightaway**.
ambition (n) (TS)	/æmˈbɪʃn/	Ehrgeiz	It's important to have **ambition**.
background (n)	/ˈbækgraʊnd/	Hintergrund	She's from a good family **background**.
bully (n)	/ˈbʊlɪ/	jmd. der einen schikaniert	You have to stand up to **bullies**.
chap (n) (TS)	/tʃæp/	Kerl	We liked Jeremy – he was a nice **chap**.
colleague (n)	/ˈkɒliːg/	Kollege, Kollegin	Do you get on with your **colleague**s?
the dark (n)	/ðə ˈdɑːk/	Dunkelheit	Are you afraid of **the dark**?
heights (n pl)	/haɪts/	große Höhen	I've always been afraid of **heights**.
music decks (n pl)	/ˈmjuːzɪk ˌdeks/	Plattenspieler	He hides behind his **music decks** at work.
prospect (n)	/ˈprɒspekt/	gute Aussichten	I want a job with **prospect**s.
social class (n)	/ˌsəʊʃl ˈklɑːs/	soziale Schicht	We're both from the same **social class**.
spider (n)	/ˈspaɪdə(r)/	Spinne	A lot of people hate **spider**s.
table manners (n pl)	/ˈteɪbl ˌmænəz/	Tischmanieren	The children have excellent **table manners**.
get on (with) (phr v)	/get ˈɒn (wɪð)/	gut auskommen (mit)	Andy doesn't **get on with** people straightaway.
give up (phr v)	/gɪv ˈʌp/	aufgeben	He **gave up** studying to be a DJ.
go for (phr v)	/ˈgəʊ fɔː(r)/	sich hingezogen fühlen zu	Do you **go for** blondes or brunettes?
go off (phr v)	/gəʊ ˈɒf/	jmd. nicht (mehr) mögen	Sarah would soon **go off** somebody who always let her do what she wants.
go out (with) (phr v)	/gəʊ ˈaʊt (wɪð)/	ein (festes) Verhältnis haben (mit)	How long have you two been **going out**?
stand up to (phr v)	/ˌstænd ˈʌp tə/	sich behaupten gegen	You have to **stand up to** bullies.
date (v)	/deɪt/	ausgehen mit	I've never **dated** anyone with red hair.
disapprove (v)	/ˌdɪsəˈpruːv/	missbilligen	Andy was worried Sarah's parents might **disapprove** of him.

6

drop (v) (TS)	/drɒp/	fallen lassen	She **dropped** Jeremy after we said we liked him!
dye (v) (TS)	/daɪ/	färben	He **dyed** his hair pink.
fancy (v)	/'fænsɪ/	etwas gern tun	She **fancies** going to London for the day.
all walks of life	/ɔːl wɔːks əv 'laɪf/	alle Schichten der Bevölkerung	I like meeting people from **all walks of life**.
be attracted to	/bi: ə'træktəd tə/	sich hingezogen fühlen zu	What sort of people **are** you **attracted to**?
be unlikely to	/bi: ʌn'laɪklɪ tə/	unwahrscheinlich sein	The poor chap **is unlikely to** last very long!
feel like (doing sth)	/'fi:l laɪk (du:ɪŋ sʌmθɪŋ)/	Lust haben zu	She **felt like having** Sunday lunch at home.
for a while (TS)	/fər ə 'waɪl/	eine Weile	Sarah and Andy have been going out **for a while**.
get bored with	/get 'bɔːd wɪð/	etwas überdrüssig sein	I **got bored with** piano lessons.
half a dozen (TS)	/hɑːf ə 'dʌzn/	ungefähr ein halbes Dutzend	We've met **half a dozen** of her boyfriends.
lose interest in	/lu:z 'ɪntrəst ɪn/	das Interesse verlieren an	People sometimes **lose interest in** their food when they're depressed.
over the years (TS)	/əʊvə ðə 'jɪəz/	mit der Zeit	**Over the years** we've met several of her boyfriends.

Do come in/Correspondence (p. 22–23)

delighted (adj)	/dɪ'laɪtəd/	entzückt	I'm **delighted** to be in touch with you.
exhausted (adj)	/ɪg'zɔːstəd/	erschöpft	Are you all right? You look **exhausted**.
grateful (adj)	/'greɪtfl/	dankbar	I would be **grateful** if you could tell me more about yourself.
reverse (adj)	/rɪ'vɜːs/	rückwärtig	Our names are on the **reverse** side of the photos.
shattered (adj)	/'ʃætəd/	wie erschlagen	They felt **shattered** after the long journey.
consequently (adv)	/'kɒnsɪkwəntlɪ/	deswegen	My best friend's been really upset; **consequently** I've been trying to cheer her up.
incidentally (adv)	/ˌɪnsɪ'dentlɪ/	übrigens	**Incidentally**, I agree with what you say about e-mail.
back roads (n pl)	/'bækrəʊdz/	Nebenstraßen	We decided to avoid the motorway and take the **back roads**.
delay (n)	/dɪ'leɪ/	Verspätung	I apologise for the **delay** in replying.
drive (n)	/draɪv/	Fahrt	The **drive** took five and a half hours.
cheer up (phr v)	/tʃɪə(r) 'ʌp/	aufmuntern	I've been trying to **cheer** my friend **up**.
chill out (phr v)	/tʃɪl 'aʊt/	entspannen	Let's just **chill out** this evening.
split up (with) (phr v)	/splɪt 'ʌp (wɪð)/	sich trennen (von)	She's just **split up with** her boyfriend.
enclose (v)	/ɪn'kləʊz/	beifügen	I **enclose** a photograph of me and my sister.
regret (v)	/rɪ'gret/	bedauern	I **regret** to inform you that I shall be unable to attend.
As for me ...	/æz fə 'mi:/	Was mich angeht	**As for me**, I'm from a very large family.
be in touch (with)	/bi: ɪn 'tʌtʃ (wɪð)/	in Kontakt bleiben (mit)	It's nice to **be in touch** with you.
be up to one's eyes in	/bi: ʌp tə wʌnz 'aɪz ɪn/	bis über die Ohren in etw. stecken	**I'm up to my eyes in** work at the moment.
by the way	/ˌbaɪ ðə 'weɪ/	übrigens	Don't forget to send a photo, **by the way**.
How's it going?	/ˌhaʊz ɪt 'gəʊɪŋ/	Wie geht's?	'**How's it going**, Andy?' 'Not too bad.'
I'm afraid that ...	/ˌaɪm ə'freɪd ðət/	Ich fürchte, dass	**I'm afraid that** I don't have a recent photo.
be on its last legs	/ɒn ɪts lɑːst 'legz/	aus dem letzten Loch pfeifen	Sadly, my car's now **on its last legs**.

English	Pronunciation	German	Example
on the back (of)	/ˈɒn ðə ˈbæk (əv)/	auf der Rückseite (von)	Our names are **on the back** of the photos.
What've you been up to?	/ˈwɒtəv jə bɪn ˈʌp tə/	Was hast du gemacht?	**What've you been up to** recently, then?
With reference to …	/wɪð ˈrefrəns tə/	In Bezug auf …	**With reference to** your letter of 12th April …
who's who	/ˌhuːz ˈhuː/	wer wer ist	Put the names on the back then I'll know **who's who**.

Unit 3

Gold fever (p. 24–25)

English	Pronunciation	German	Example
disillusioned (adj)	/ˌdɪsɪˈluːʒnd/	enttäuscht	Sutter left California **disillusioned**.
distant (adj)	/ˈdɪstənt/	entlegen	In 1839 California was a **distant** outpost.
epic (adj)	/ˈepɪk/	lang und abenteuerlich	Thousands of people made the **epic** journey west.
joint (adj)	/dʒɔɪnt/	zusammengeschlossen	People formed **joint** stock companies.
ruined (adj)	/ˈruːɪnd/	ruiniert	By 1850 Sutter was a **ruined** man.
unnoticed (adj)	/ʌnˈnəʊtɪst/	unbeachtet	Brannan eventually died an **unnoticed** death.
eastward (adv)	/ˈiːstwəd/	ostwärts	Rumours of a gold strike drifted **eastward** across the country.
entirely (adv)	/ɪnˈtaɪəlɪ/	völlig	When they would return was another matter **entirely**.
keenly (adv)	/ˈkiːnlɪ/	deutlich	Brannan **keenly** understood the situation.
adventurer (n)	/ədˈventʃərə(r)/	Abenteurer	Thousands of young **adventurer**s came looking for gold.
alcoholism (n)	/ˈælkəhɒlɪzm/	Alkoholismus	**Alcoholism** led to Brannan's death.
building materials (n pl)	/ˈbɪldɪŋ məˌtɪərɪəlz/	Baumaterial	The Forty-Niners destroyed Sutter's fort for **building materials**.
cattle (n)	/ˈkætl/	Stück Vieh	Sutter had 12,000 **cattle**.
a deluge of (n)	/ə ˈdeljuːdʒ əv/	eine Flut von	**A deluge of** humanity arrived in California.
downfall (n)	/ˈdaʊnfɔːl/	Untergang	Alcoholism led to Brannan's **downfall**.
empire (n)	/ˈempaɪə(r)/	Reich	Sutter wanted to build his own private **empire**.
epidemic (n)	/epɪˈdemɪk/	Epidemie	In 1849 gold fever was an **epidemic**.
glint (n)	/glɪnt/	Glitzern	Marshall saw a **glint** of gold in the ground.
gold fever (n)	/ˈɡəʊld ˌfiːvə(r)/	Goldfieber	**'Gold fever'** descended on the whole country.
gold fields (n)	/ˈɡəʊld ˌfiːldz/	Goldfelder	Brannan owned the only store between San Francisco and the **gold field**s.
gold rush (n)	/ˈɡəʊld ˌrʌʃ/	Goldrausch	During the **gold rush** Sam Brannan became extremely wealthy.
gold strike (n)	/ˈɡəʊld ˌstraɪk/	Goldfund	Rumours of a **gold strike** spread quickly.
a handful of (n)	/ə ˈhændfʊl əv/	eine Handvoll	Only **a handful of** Americans had been to California in 1839.
humanity (n)	/hjuːˈmænətɪ/	Menschen	The flood of **humanity** destroyed Sutter's dream.
kingdom (n)	/ˈkɪŋdəm/	Königreich	Sutter saw the newcomers as subjects for his **kingdom**.
lifetime (n)	/ˈlaɪftaɪm/	Menschenleben	The Forty-Niners thought they would earn a **lifetime** of riches.
newcomer (n)	/ˈnjuːkʌmə(r)/	Neuling	Sutter welcomed the **newcomer**s at first.

outpost (n)	/ˈaʊtpəʊst/	Außenstelle	California was just a distant **outpost**.
pan (n)	/pæn/	Pfanne	**Pans** are used for washing gold.
persecution (n) (TS)	/ˌpɜːsɪˈkjuːʃn/	Verfolgung	Brannan left New York to escape religious **persecution**.
pick (n)	/pɪk/	Pickel	**Picks** are used for digging in the ground for gold.
possessions (n pl)	/pəˈzeʃənz/	Besitz	People sold their **possession**s to make the journey west.
riches (n pl)	/ˈrɪtʃɪz/	Reichtum	The Forty-Niners hoped to make a lifetime of **riches**.
risk-taker (n)	/ˈrɪskteɪkə(r)/	jmd., der Risiken eingeht	Sutter and Brannan were both **risk-taker**s.
sawmill (n)	/ˈsɔːmɪl/	Sägemühle	They built a **sawmill** on the American River.
shovel (n)	/ˈʃʌvl/	Schaufel	Brannan bought all the picks and **shovel**s he could find.
statement (n)	/ˈsteɪtmənt/	Erklärung	President Polk made a **statement** to Congress about the discovery.
stock company (n)	/ˈstɒk ˌkʌmpənɪ/	Gesellschaft	Some of the adventurers formed **stock compan**ies.
subject (n)	/ˈsʌbdʒekt/	Untertan	Sutter saw the newcomers as **subject**s for his new kingdom.
trickle (n)	/ˈtrɪkl/	Bächlein	The **trickle** of people eventually became a flood.
whispers (of) (n pl)	/ˈwɪspəz (əv)/	Gerüchte (über)	**Whispers** of a gold strike spread across the country.
band together (phr v)	/ˌbænd təˈgeðə(r)/	sich vereinigen	People **banded together** to form stock companies.
capitalise on (phr v)	/ˈkæpɪtəlaɪz ˌɒn/	profitieren von	Sutter never **capitalised on** the discovery of gold.
descend on (phr v)	/dɪˈsend ɒn/	kommen über	Gold fever soon **descended on** the country.
end up with (phr v)	/end ˈʌp wɪð/	enden mit	Brannan **ended up with** a lot more gold than the diggers!
pick up (phr v)	/ˌpɪk ˈʌp/	aufheben	Marshall **picked up** a small piece of gold.
reach down (phr v)	/ˌriːtʃ ˈdaʊn/	hinunterfassen	He **reached down** and picked up a piece of gold.
tear down (phr v)	/ˌteə ˈdaʊn/	abbrechen	The Forty-Niners **tore down** Sutter's fort.
alter (v)	/ˈɑːltə(r)/	verändern	Sutter refused to **alter** his vision.
benefit (v) (TS)	/ˈbenɪfɪt/	aus einer Sache Profit schlagen	Many of those who **benefited** from the gold rush eventually lost their fortune.
dig (v) (TS)	/dɪg/	graben	Brannan had no intention of **digging** for gold.
drift (v)	/drɪft/	treiben	Rumours of the gold strike **drifted** eastward.
mortgage (v)	/ˈmɔːgɪdʒ/	verpfänden	Thousands of people **mortgaged** their farms.
stream (v)	/striːm/	strömen	People **streamed** west in search of gold.
telegraph (v)	/ˈtelɪgrɑːf/	telegrafieren	The news was **telegraphed** to every village and town.
thump (v)	/θʌmp/	klopfen	The discovery made Marshall's heart **thump**.
trample (v)	/ˈtræmpl/	zertrampeln	Sutter's crops were **trampled**.
triple (v) (TS)	/ˈtrɪpl/	verdreifachen	Brannan and his companions **tripled** San Francisco's population.
welcome (v)	/ˈwelkəm/	Willkommen heißen	At first Sutter **welcomed** the newcomers.
another matter	/bi: əˈnʌðə ˈmætə(r)/	eine andere Sache	When the Forty-Niners would return was **another matter**.
be in the way	/bi: ɪn ðə ˈweɪ/	im Weg stehen	In the new California Sutter **was** simply **in the way**.
be intent on	/ˌbi: ɪnˈtent ɒn/	hinter etwas her sein	He **was intent on** building his own empire.
catch sb's eye	/ˈkætʃ sʌmbɑdɪz ˈaɪ/	Aufmerksamkeit auf sich lenken	A glint of gold **caught Marshall's eye**.
corner the market	/ˌkɔːnə ðə ˈmɑːkɪt/	den Markt beherrschen	Brannan successfully **cornered the market**.

English	Pronunciation	German	Example
a gap in the market	/ə ˌgæp ɪn ðə ˈmɑːkɪt/	Marktlücke	He recognised **a gap in the market**.
have a go at	/ˌhæv ə ˈgəʊ ət/	etwas ausprobieren	I'd like to **have a go at** skiing.
have a think (about)	/ˈhæv ə ˈθɪŋk (əˈbaʊt)/	sich Gedanken machen (über)	I need time to **have a think** about it.
in return for	/ɪn rɪˈtɜːn fə(r)/	im Tausch für	They thought they would have a year of pain **in return for** a lifetime of riches.
the laws of supply and demand (TS)	/ðə ˌlɔːz əv səˈplaɪ ən dɪˈmɑːnd/	das Gesetz von Angebot und Nachfrage	Brannan understood **the laws of supply and demand**.
make a mess of	/ˌmeɪk ə ˈmes əv/	vermasseln	She **made a mess of** her exams.
make money	/ˌmeɪk ˈmʌnɪ/	Geld verdienen	All he's interested in is **making money**.
make sense	/ˌmeɪk ˈsens/	einen Sinn ergeben	I don't understand this – it just doesn't **make sense**.
run up and down (TS)	/ˌrʌn ˌʌp ən ˈdaʊn/	hin- und herrennen	He **ran up and down** the street shouting.
say one's goodbyes	/ˌseɪ wʌnz gʊdˈbaɪz/	sich verabschieden	It's time to **say our goodbyes**.
take a chance on	/ˌteɪk ə ˈtʃɑːns ɒn/	sein Glück versuchen	The adventurers were willing to **take a chance on** gold.
take advantage of	/ˌteɪk ədˈvɑːntɪdʒ əv/	etwas benutzen	You should **take advantage of** every opportunity.
half-baked (adj)	/hɑːfˈbeɪkt/	unausgegoren	I promise you it's not some **half-baked** idea.
proper (adj)	/ˈprɒpə(r)/	richtig	You should concentrate on getting a **proper** job.
profitably (adv)	/ˈprɒfɪtəblɪ/	nutzbringend	Try to use your time more **profitably**.
triumphantly (adv)	/traɪˈʌmfəntlɪ/	triumphierend	'You could spend all your time on the beach,' said the tourist **triumphantly**.
click (n)	/klɪk/	Klicken	The **click** of the camera woke the fisherman up.
decision-making (n)	/dɪˈsɪʒn ˌmeɪkɪŋ/	Entscheidungen treffen	Don't rush **decision-making**.
fishing boat (n)	/ˈfɪʃɪŋ ˈbəʊt/	Fischerboot	The man was dozing in his **fishing boat**.
fleet (n)	/fliːt/	Flotte	If you saved enough money you could have a **fleet** of fishing boats.
wisdom (n)	/ˈwɪzdəm/	Weisheit	Is **wisdom** more precious than youth?
youth (n)	/juːθ/	Jugend	... or is **youth** more precious than wisdom?
chew over (phr v)	/ˈtʃuː ˌəʊvə(r)/	nachdenken	I've been **chewing over** the idea for weeks.
lie around (phr v)	/ˌlaɪ əˈraʊnd/	faulenzen	He enjoys **lying around** in the sun.
think through (phr v)	/ˌθɪŋk ˈθruː/	nachdenken über	Give me time to think it **through**.
use up (phr v)	/ˌjuːz ˈʌp/	aufbrauchen	All the best ideas have been **used up**.
digest (v)	/daɪˈdʒest/	verarbeiten	I need time to **digest** the information.
doze (v)	/dəʊz/	dösen	The man was **dozing** in a fishing boat.
waste (v)	/weɪst/	verschwenden	Stop **wasting** time!
be worth one's while	/bɪ ˌwɜːθ wʌnz ˈwaɪl/	sich lohnen	Just listen to me – it'll **be worth your while**.
food for thought	/ˌfuːd fə ˈθɔːt/	Stoff zum Nachdenken	Serious books give you **food for thought**.

Money talks/Close up (p. 29–30)

English	Pronunciation	German	Example
broke (adj)	/brəʊk/	pleite	When I was a student I was always **broke**.
hand-painted (adj)	/ˈhænd ˌpeɪntəd/	handbemalt	I had a set of **hand-painted** toy soldiers.
massive (adj)	/ˈmæsɪv/	enorm	I'd buy a set of **massive** speakers for my stereo.

breadwinner (n)	/ˈbredwɪnə(r)/	Hauptverdiener	His wife's the main **breadwinner** in their house.
charity (n)	/ˈtʃærəti/	Wohltätigkeit	Have you ever given money to **charity**?
failure (n) (TS)	/ˈfeɪljə(r)/	Misserfolg	I'd feel like a **failure** if my wife earned more than me.
human nature (n) (TS)	/ˌhjuːmən ˈneɪtʃə(r)/	die Natur des Menschen	It's only **human nature** to feel jealous from time to time.
overdraft (n) (TS)	/ˈəʊvədrɑːft/	Bankschulden	The sensible thing would be to pay off my **overdraft**.
pocket money (n)	/ˈpɒkɪt ˌmʌni/	Taschengeld	Do your parents give you **pocket money**?
speakers (n pl)	/ˈspiːkəz/	Lautsprecher	I'd buy a new set of **speakers**.
stereo system (n)	/ˈsteriəʊ ˌsɪstəm/	Stereoanlage	Do you own a **stereo system**?
blow sth on sth (phr v)	/ˈbləʊ sʌmθɪŋ ɒn sʌmθɪŋ/	ausgeben für	Alan **blew all the money on a weekend** in New York.
name sth after sb (phr v)	/ˌneɪm sʌmθɪŋ ˈɑːftə(r) sʌmbədiz/	etwas nach jmd. benennen	Would you ever have a famous building **named after you**?
pay off (phr v) (TS)	/ˈpeɪ ˌɒf/	abzahlen	Have you managed to **pay off** your overdraft?
save up (for) (phr v)	/ˌseɪv ˈʌp (fə(r))/	sparen (auf)	We're **saving up** for a new car.
splash out (on) (phr v)	/splæʃ ˈaʊt (ɒn)/	sich etw. spendieren	I'd love to **splash out** on some new clothes.
appoint (v)	/əˈpɔɪnt/	ernennen	If you were president, who would you **appoint** as your ministers?
ban (v)	/bæn/	verbieten	I'd **ban** smoking in public places.
behave oneself (v)	/bɪˈheɪv wʌnself/	sich benehmen	You won't get any pocket money unless you **behave yourself**.
inherit (v)	/ɪnˈherɪt/	erben	She **inherited** some money from her grandmother.
be tempted to do sth (TS)	/bɪ ˌtemptəd tə ˈduː sʌmθɪŋ/	in Versuchung geraten zu	Eric would **be tempted to buy** a new computer.
be worth a fortune	/bɪ ˌwɜːθ ə ˈfɔːtʃuːn/	ein Vermögen wert sein	That house must **be worth a fortune**.
earn a fortune	/ˌɜːn ə ˈfɔːtʃuːn/	ein Vermögen verdienen	Lawyers **earn a fortune**.
earn a living (TS)	/ˌɜːn ə ˈlɪvɪŋ/	sein Brot verdienen	Do you agree that it's a man's job to **earn a living**?
fame or fortune	/ˌfeɪm ɔː ˈfɔːtʃuːn/	Ruhm oder Reichtum	Would you prefer **fame or fortune**?
loads of (TS)	/ˈləʊdz əv/	ein Haufen	I know **loads of** couples where the woman is the main breadwinner.
Lucky thing!	/ˌlʌki ˈθɪŋ/	Glückspilz	'Alan won £2000.' '**Lucky thing**.'
on condition that	/ɒn kənˈdɪʃn θət/	unter der Bedingung, dass	He gave me pocket money **on condition that** I behaved myself.
save it for a rainy day	/ˌseɪv ɪt fə(r) ə ˌreɪni ˈdeɪ/	etwas auf die Seite legen	I'm not spending the money – I'm **saving it for a rainy day**.
take a year out	/ˌteɪk ə jɪə(r) ˈaʊt/	ein Jahr frei nehmen	A lot of students now **take a year out** between school and university.

Treasured possessions/A day in my very wealthy life (p. 32–33)

frantically (adv) (TS)	/ˈfræntɪkli/	verzweifelt	She tried **frantically** to find a way out of the avalanche.
greatly (adv) (TS)	/ˈɡreɪtli/	sehr	Treasured possessions are things that people value **greatly**.
luckily (adv) (TS)	/ˈlʌkəli/	glücklicherweise	**Luckily** the others found Heather in the avalanche.
admirer (n)	/ədˈmaɪrə(r)/	Verehrer	He got a present from a secret **admirer**.
bedside table (n)	/ˌbedsaɪd ˈteɪbl/	Nachtschränkchen	Katie keeps her mother's wedding ring on her **bedside table**.
composer (n)	/kəmˈpəʊzə(r)/	Komponist	Armando's father was a **composer**.
crack (n) (TS)	/kræk/	Knall	She heard a loud **crack** and then the snow began to fall.

details (n pl) (TS)	/ˈdiːteɪlz/	Einzelheiten	Mike's mobile phone contains the **details** of about 300 people.
housekeeper (n)	/ˈhaʊskiːpə(r)/	Haushälter(in)	My **housekeeper** prepares my breakfast.
museum piece (n) (TS)	/mjuːˈzɪəm piːs/	Museumsstück	Armando's typewriter is now a **museum piece**.
neck-warmer (n)	/ˈnekwɔːmə(r)/	Nackenwärmer	Heather's **neck-warmer** saved her life.
storyteller (n)	/ˈstɔːrɪtelə(r)/	Erzähler	Armando's father was a **storyteller**.
tracks (n pl) (TS)	/træks/	Fußspuren	We followed the **tracks** of the first person.
treasured possession (n)	/ˌtreʒəd pəˈzeʃn/	kostbarer Besitz (für einen persönlich)	What's your most **treasured possession**?
sweep up (phr v) (TS)	/ˌswiːp ˈʌp/	mitreißen	The avalanche just **swept** me **up**.
acquire (v)	/əˈkwaɪə(r)/	erwerben	How did you **acquire** your most treasured possession?
leap (v) (TS)	/liːp/	springen	The first person in the group **leapt** off the cornice.
settle (v) (TS)	/ˈsetl/	sich legen	When the snow **settled** I pushed my glove through the surface.
be starving	/bɪ ˈstɑːvɪŋ/	sehr hungrig sein	When I met my friend at the restaurant I **was starving**.
by the time	/ˌbaɪ ðə ˈtaɪm/	bis	**By the time** I met my friend at the restaurant I was starving.
just as	/ˈdʒʌst əz/	gerade als	**Just as** we were leaving the restaurant, I spotted someone I'd always wanted to meet.
stay aware (TS)	/ˌsteɪ əˈweə(r)/	sich bewusst bleiben	I tried to **stay aware** of which direction I was going in.
the main thing is (TS)	/ðə ˈmeɪn θɪŋ ɪz/	das Wichtigste ist	**The main thing is** that if I lost this, I'd lose the addresses of 300 people.

Unit 4

Sympathy and advice (p. 34–35)

raw (adj) (TS)	/rɔː/	roh	Mix a couple of **raw** eggs in a cup..
cure (n)	/kjʊə(r)/	Heilmittel	I know a secret **cure** for hangovers.
ginger (n) (TS)	/ˈdʒɪndʒə(r)/	Ingwer	Chop up some **ginger** and put it in boiling water.
hangover (n)	/ˈhæŋəʊvə(r)/	Kater	I had too much to drink last night and now I've got a terrible **hangover**.
hayfever (n)	/ˈheɪfiːvə(r)/	Heuschnupfen	A lot of people get **hayfever** in the summer.
sunburn (n)	/ˈsʌnbɜːn/	Sonnenbrand	Greg's got dreadful **sunburn**.
swelling (n) (TS)	/ˈswelɪŋ/	Schwellung	Ice will help to reduce the **swelling**.
tan (n)	/tæn/	Sonnenbräune	Greg wanted to get a **tan** quickly.
bring on (phr v) (TS)	/brɪŋ ˈɒn/	verursachen	Headaches are often **brought on** by sitting in front of a computer for too long.
chop up (phr v) (TS)	/tʃɒp ˈʌp/	zerkleinern	**Chop up** some ginger and put it in boiling water.
drink down (phr v) (TS)	/drɪŋk ˈdaʊn/	auf einen Zug leeren	You have to **drink** it all **down** in one go.
mix up (phr v) (TS)	/mɪks ˈʌp/	vermengen	**Mix** all the ingredients **up**.
sting (v)	/stɪŋ/	stechen	My back really **stings**.
a heavy night	/ə ˌhevi ˈnaɪt/	harter Abend	Bob had a **heavy night** and drank too much.
a pinch of (TS)	/ə ˈpɪntʃ əv/	eine Prise	Add some chilli sauce and **a pinch of** salt.

a splitting headache	/ə ˌsplɪtɪŋ ˈhedeɪk/	rasende Kopfschmerzen	Staring at a computer screen for long periods can give you **a splitting headache**.
a streaming nose	/ə ˌstriːmɪŋ ˈnəʊz/	eine Triefnase	I get red eyes and **a streaming nose**.
a twisted ankle	/ə ˌtwɪstɪd ˈæŋkl/	verstauchter Knöchel	'Why are you walking like that?' 'I've got **a twisted ankle**.'
if you ask me (TS)	/ɪf juː ˌɑːsk ˈmiː/	meiner Meinung nach	**If you ask me**, you need to lie down and rest.
in one go (TS)	/ɪn ˌwʌn ˈgəʊ/	auf einmal	Try to drink it **in one go**.
It hasn't worked.	/ɪt ˌhæznt ˈwɜːkt/	Es hat nicht gewirkt.	I've taken an aspirin but **it hasn't worked**.
It serves you right.	/ɪt ˌsɜːvz jə ˈraɪt/	Das gescheiht dir recht.	'I didn't put any suntan lotion on.' 'Oh well, **it serves you right**.'
It's killing me.	/ɪts ˈkɪlɪŋ miː/	Es tut höllisch weh.	My ankle's **killing me**.
look like death warmed up	/lʊk laɪk ˌdeθ wɔːmd ˈʌp/	hundeelend aussehen	Bob felt terrible and **looked like death warmed up**.
You've only got yourself to blame.	/jəv ˌəʊnlɪ gɒt ˌjaself tə ˈbleɪm/	Du bist selber schuld.	'I've been playing computer games for seven hours.' 'Well, **you've only got yourself to blame**, haven't you?'

Body knowledge/Close up (p. 35–36)

following (adj)	/ˈfɒləʊɪŋ/	folgend	Which of the **following** activites are best for keeping supple? Yoga or wind-surfing.
high (adj) (TS)	/haɪ/	toll	After you've had a good work-out you feel **high**.
run down (adj)	/rʌn ˈdaʊn/	übermüdet	Exercise makes you feel better when you're feeling **run down**.
supple (adj)	/ˈsʌpl/	gelenkig	Yoga is a great way of keeping **supple**.
aerobic system (n)	/eəˈrəʊbɪk ˌsɪstəm/	Atemorgane	The **aerobic system** is the heart, lungs and blood circulation.
balanced diet (n)	/ˌbælənst ˈdaɪət/	eine ausgewogene Ernährung	It's important to eat a **balanced diet**.
rowing (n)	/ˈrəʊɪŋ/	Rudern	**Rowing** helps to build up your muscles.
stamina (n)	/ˈstæmɪnə/	Ausdauer	Regular exercise helps you to build up **stamina**.
suppleness (n)	/ˈsʌplnəs/	Gelenkigkeit	Yoga improves the **suppleness** of your body.
work-out (n) (TS)	/ˈwɜːkaʊt/	Training	I always feel better after a **work-out** at the gym.
build up (phr v)	/ˌbɪld ˈʌp/	aufbauen	Exercising regularly **builds up** stamina.
cut down (on) (phr v)	/ˌkʌt ˈdaʊn (ɒn)/	etwas einschränken	Try to **cut down on** sugar and caffeine.
slob out (phr v)	/ˌslɒb ˈaʊt/	auf der faulen Haut liegen	She spends too much time **slobbing out** in front of the television.
tone up (phr v)	/ˌtəʊn ˈʌp/	kräftiger werden	I need to lose weight and **tone up**.
overdo (v)	/ˌəʊvəˈduː/	übertreiben	You shouldn't **overdo** exercise.
release (v)	/rɪˈliːs/	freisetzen	Endorphins are **released** during exercise.
snack (v)	/snæk/	eine Zwischenmahlzeit einnehmen	It's bad for you to **snack** throughout the day.
bearing in mind (that) ...	/ˌbeərɪŋ ɪn ˈmaɪnd (ðət)/	Wenn man berücksichtigt, (dass)	**Bearing in mind that** I work from 9 to 5 in an office, what do you suggest?
in good working order	/ɪn ˌgʊd ˌwɜːkɪŋ ˈɔːdə(r)/	in guter Verfassung	It's important to keep your body **in good working order**.
keep (sth) in shape	/ˌkiːp (sʌmθɪŋ) ɪn ˈʃeɪp/	in Form halten	Exercise helps **keep your body in shape**.
out of shape	/ˌaʊt əv ˈʃeɪp/	schlecht in Form	I feel depressed – I'm really **out of shape**.
take the pleasure out of sth	/ˌteɪk ðə ˈpleʒə(r) aʊt əv sʌmθɪŋ/	einer Sache den Spaß nehmen	Don't take exercise too seriously – it **takes all the pleasure out of it**.

Body language/Shape your body (p. 37–38)

best-selling (adj)	/ˌbestˈselɪŋ/	einen reißenden Absatz haben	The F-plan diet is the **best-selling** diet ever.
debatable (adj)	/dɪˈbeɪtəbl/	diskutabel	The Hay diet has a **debatable** scientific basis.
fatty (adj) (TS)	/ˈfætɪ/	fett	Meat tends to be very **fatty.**
initial (adj)	/ɪˈnɪʃl/	anfänglich	**Initial** weight-loss is due to losing water.
minute (adj) (TS)	/maɪˈnjuːt/	geringfügig	The waist is **minute**!
sugar-coated (adj)	/ˈʃʊgəkəʊtɪd/	gezuckert	The System S diet advises eating **sugar-coated** cereals.
sugary (adj)	/ˈʃʊgərɪ/	gesüßt	**Sugary** soft drinks are bad for your teeth.
well-earned (adj) (TS)	/ˌwelˈɜːnd/	wohlverdient	Sam is going to have a **well-earned** treat.
hopefully (adv) (TS)	/ˈhəʊpfəlɪ/	hoffentlich	**Hopefully,** I won't need to wear the wedding dress again!
non-stop (adv) (TS)	/ˌnɒnˈstɒp/	ununterbrochen	Sam has been training **non-stop** for ages.
absorption (n)	/əbˈsɔːpʃn/	Aufnahme	Vitamin C helps the body's **absorption** of iron.
artery (n)	/ˈɑːtərɪ/	Arterie	Eating large amounts of fat is bad for your **arteries**.
basis (n)	/ˈbeɪsɪs/	Grundlage	There's not much scientific **basis** for the Hay diet.
breakthrough (n)	/ˈbreɪkθruː/	Durchbruch	The F-plan diet was supposed to be a scientific **breakthrough**.
common sense (n)	/ˌkɒmən ˈsens/	gesunder Menschenverstand	Basically, the F-plan diet is **common sense**.
dairy products (n pl)	/ˈdeərɪ ˌprɒdʌkts/	Molkereiprodukte	Milk and cheese are **dairy products**.
energy levels (n pl) (TS)	/ˈenədʒɪ ˌlevəlz/	Leistungsniveau	You have to increase your **energy levels** for kick-boxing.
heart disease (n)	/ˈhɑːt dɪziːz/	Herz-Kreislauf-Erkrankung	Eating fat is linked to **heart disease**.
main meal (n)	/ˌmeɪn ˈmiːl/	Hauptmahlzeit	What time of day do you have your **main meal**?
metabolism (n)	/məˈtæbəlɪzm/	Stoffwechsel	A mixture of foods is necessary for a healthy **metabolism**.
premise (n)	/ˈpremɪs/	Annahme	What **premise** is the diet based on?
side effect (n)	/ˈsaɪd ɪfekt/	Nebenwirkung	The cabbage soup diet can lead to **side effects**.
sit-up (n) (TS)	/ˈsɪtʌp/	Bauchmuskelübung	Catherine hated doing **sit-up**s every morning.
treat (n) (TS)	/triːt/	Leckerbissen	Sam deserves a **treat** after training so hard.
villain (n)	/ˈvɪlən/	Übeltäter	The System S diet says that sweets and chocolate aren't the **villain**s they're made out to be.
weight-gain (n)	/ˈweɪtgeɪn/	Gewichtszunahme	Do large amounts of carbohydrate lead to **weight-gain**?
weight-lifting (n) (TS)	/ˈweɪtlɪftɪŋ/	Gewichtheben	Sam doesn't do too much **weight-lifting**.
weight-loss (n)	/ˈweɪtlɒs/	Gewichtsverlust	The aim of any diet is **weight-loss**.
move back (on to) (phr v)	/ˈmuːv bæk ɒn tə/	zurückkehren (zu)	You put on weight again when you **move back on to** solids.
stick to (phr v) (TS)	/ˈstɪk tə/	sich halten an	Sam tries to **stick to** fish and not eat too much meat.
tuck into (phr v)	/ˈtʌk ɪn ˌtə/	zulangen bei	According to the System S diet you can **tuck into** sweets and chocolate.
disguise (v)	/dɪsˈgaɪz/	verkappen	The F-plan diet is common sense **disguised** as a scientific breakthrough.
reshape (v) (TS)	/riːˈʃeɪp/	neu formen	Some Hollywood actors have plastic surgery to **reshape** their bodies.
rot (v)	/rɒt/	verfaulen	Sweets **rot** your teeth.

a night out (TS)	/ə ˌnaɪt 'aʊt/	ein Abend aus	I'm having **a night out** to celebrate.
a shoulder to cry on	/ə ˈʃəʊldə tə ˈkraɪ ɒn/	eine Schulter zum Ausweinen	We all need **a shoulder to cry on** from time to time.
a vast amount of	/ə ˌvɑːst əˈmaʊnt əv/	eine enorme Menge	You'd have to eat **a vast amount of** celery for this diet to make any difference.
be dying for (TS)	/bɪ ˈdaɪɪŋ fə(r)/	sich sehnen nach	I **was dying for** a nice plate of spaghetti!
be on one's way to	/biː ɒn wʌnz ˈweɪ tə/	unterwegs sein zu/nach	Laura **was on her way to** the third meeting of the day.
for instance	/fə(r) ˈɪnstəns/	zum Beispiel	Vitamin C **for instance,** helps the absorption of iron.
get it off one's chest	/ɡet ɪt ɒf wʌnz ˈtʃest/	seinem Herzen Luft machen	If you're worried about something it's best to **get it off your chest**.
get rid of (TS)	/ɡet ˈrɪd əv/	etwas loswerden	She wanted to **get rid of** her stomach.
go through hell (TS)	/ɡəʊ θruː ˈhel/	Fürchterliches durchmachen	Catherine had to **go through hell** to lose weight before the wedding.
have one's fingers in a lot of pies	/hæv wʌnz ˈfɪŋɡəz ɪn ə lɒt əv ˈpaɪz/	überall seine Finger im Spiel haben	He owns several companies and **has his fingers in a lot of pies**.
make sth out to be sth	/meɪk sʌmθɪŋ ˈaʊt tə bɪ sʌmθɪŋ/	jmd. darstellen als	Do you agree that sweet foods are not necessarily **the villains** they're **made out to be**?
play it by ear	/ˌpleɪ ɪt baɪ ˈɪə(r)/	improvisieren	'Are you going on holiday, then?' 'I'm going to **play it by ear**.'
put one's foot in it	/pʊt wʌnz ˈfʊt ɪn ɪt/	ins Fettnäpfchen treten	I **put my foot in it** by asking Phil about his girlfriend.
strictly forbidden	/ˌstrɪklɪ fəˈbɪdən/	strengstens untersagt	In the Hay diet mixing acid and alkaline is **strictly forbidden**.
this neck of the woods	/ðɪs ˌnek əv ðə ˈwʊdz/	diese Gegend	You wouldn't know her – she's not from **this neck of the woods**.
Trust me to ...	/trʌst ˈmiː tə/	Verlass sich drauf, dass ich ...	**Trust me to** say something stupid!
when the time comes	/wen ðə ˌtaɪm ˈkʌmz/	wenn es soweit ist	I'll decide whether or not I'm going to go away **when the time comes**.

I will quit. Soon./Close up (p. 39–40)

hooked (adj)	/hʊkt/	süchtig	Once you've started smoking it's easy to get **hooked**.
intact (adj)	/ɪnˈtækt/	ganz	To his delight he found the cigarettes were **intact**.
nasty (adj)	/ˈnɑːstɪ/	unangenehm	Smoking is a **nasty** habit.
relieved (adj)	/rɪˈliːvd/	erleichtert	I was **relieved** no one answered the phone.
steadily (adv)	/ˈstedɪlɪ/	beständig	Slowly but **steadily** I had become hooked.
whenever (adv)	/wenˈevə(r)/	egal wann	Call me **whenever**.
bloke (n)	/bləʊk/	Kerl	He picked up the technique from a **bloke** in Russia.
desire (n)	/dɪˈzaɪə(r)/	Verlangen	Call me when you feel the **desire** to smoke.
doorstep (n)	/ˈdɔːstep/	Schwelle	He was standing on Shubentsov's office **doorstep**.
fingertips (n pl)	/ˈfɪŋɡətɪps/	Fingerspitzen	Shubentsov transmits healing energy from his **fingertips**.
quitting technique (n)	/ˈkwɪtɪŋ tekˌniːk/	Methode, um aufzuhören	I've tried all the **quitting technique**s.
urge (n)	/ɜːdʒ/	Drang	The **urge** to smoke is difficult to resist.
chase away (phr v)	/tʃeɪs əˈweɪ/	verjagen	Cigarette smoke will **chase away** mosquitoes.
come over (phr v)	/kʌm ˈəʊvə(r)/	überkommen	A strange feeling **came over** me.
count on (phr v)	/ˈkaʊnt ɒn/	sich verlassen	He's very reliable – you can **count on** him.
drive away (phr v)	/ˌdraɪv əˈweɪ/	wegjagen	Smoking can help **drive away** annoying people.
get over (phr v)	/ɡet ˈəʊvə(r)/	etwas überstehen	Cigarettes have helped me **get over** losses.

hop down (phr v)	/ˌhɒp ˈdaʊn/	hinunterspringen	I **hopped down** from the doorstep to pick them up.
let down (phr v)	/ˌlet ˈdaʊn/	im Stich lassen	Cigarettes have never **let** me **down**.
light up (phr v)	/ˌlaɪt ˈʌp/	anzünden	He couldn't resist the urge to **light up**.
look into (phr v)	/ˌlʊk ˈɪntə/	untersuchen	We're **looking into** these complaints.
pick up from (phr v)	/ˌpɪk ˈʌp frəm/	von jmd. etwas lernen	Shubentsov **picked up** the technique **from** another bloke in Russia.
see through (phr v)	/ˌsiː ˈθruː/	jmd. durchschauen	I **saw through** her immediately and knew she was lying.
claim (v)	/kleɪm/	behaupten	A lot of people **claim** to smoke for pleasure.
comfort (v)	/ˈkʌmfət/	trösten	Smoking has **comforted** me on many occasions.
cure (v)	/kjʊə(r)/	heilen	Shubentsov is well known for **curing** smokers of their habit.
deceive (v)	/dɪˈsiːv/	täuschen	I wasn't **deceived** by her and knew she was lying.
dial (v)	/ˈdaɪəl/	wählen	He **dialled** Shubentsov's number.
injure (v)	/ˈɪndʒə(r)/	verletzen	My dad keeps **injuring** himself playing football.
pocket (v)	/ˈpɒkɪt/	einstecken	He picked up the packs and **pocketed** them.
quit (v)	/kwɪt/	aufhören	It's not easy to **quit** smoking.
recover (v)	/rɪˈkʌvə(r)/	sich erholen	It took me a long time to **recover** from that cold.
struggle (v)	/ˈstrʌgl/	kämpfen	A lot of people **struggle** to give up smoking.
transmit (v)	/trænsˈmɪt/	übertragen	He **transmit**s healing through his fingertips.
become clear	/bɪkʌm ˈklɪə(r)/	einleuchten	Things **became clear** later.
clear one's head	/ˌklɪə wʌnz ˈhed/	einen klaren Kopf bekommen	Smoking **clears my head**.
do one's part	/ˌduː wʌnz ˈpɑːt/	seine Pflicht erfüllen	If I try phoning I feel as if I've **done my part**.
healing energy	/ˌhiːlɪŋ ˈenədʒɪ/	heilende Kraft	I could feel Shubentsov's **healing energy**.
It dawned on me/her/him etc	/ɪt ˈdɔːnd ɒn ˌmiː/ ˌhɜː/hɪm	Es wurde mir/ihr/ihm klar	**It dawned on us** that she might still be asleep.
lose control of	/ˌluːz kənˈtrəʊl əv/	die Kontrolle über … verlieren	I realise I'm **losing control of** the habit.
Step on it!	/ˈstep ɒn ɪt/	Beeil dich!	**Step on it!** We're going to be late.
That's another story.	/ˌðæts əˌnʌðə ˈstɔːrɪ/	Das ist eine andere Geschichte.	Whether I'll enjoy the cigarette **is another story**.
The funny thing is …	/ðə ˌfʌnɪ θɪŋ ˈɪz/	merkwürdigerweise	**The funny thing is** that I'm not phoning him to stop me from lighting up.
the urge strikes	/ðiː ˌɜːdʒ ˈstraɪks/	der Drang überkommt jmd.	Any time **the urge** to smoke **strikes**, just give me a call.
to my delight	/tə ˌmaɪ dɪˈlaɪt/	zu meiner Freude	**To my delight**, all the cigarettes were intact.

Unit 5
Football mad! (p. 42–44)

live (adj)	/laɪv/	direkt übertragen	Do you ever watch **live** football on TV?
oncoming (adj)	/ˈɒnkʌmɪŋ/	entgegen kommend	They used to throw the sugar mouse heads under the wheels of **oncoming** cars.
unbeaten (adj)	/ʌnˈbiːtn/	unbesiegt	If they performed this ritual every week they hoped United would remain **unbeaten**.

growing-up (n)	/ˈɡrəʊɪŋˈʌp/	Heranwachsen	Hornby's novels are about obsession and **growing-up**.
injury time (n)	/ˈɪndʒəri ˌtaɪm/	Nachspiel	Terry was ecstatic when Man Utd scored the winner in **injury time**.
kick-off (n)	/ˈkɪkɒf/	Anstoß	**Kick-off** is at 3 pm.
torso (n)	/ˈtɔːsəʊ/	Körper	The sugar mouse **torso**s were tossed in the road.
turnstile (n)	/ˈtɜːnstaɪl/	Drehkreuz	He always used to enter the stadium through the same **turnstile**.
bite off (phr v)	/ˌbaɪt ˈɒf/	abbeißen	They used to **bite** the head **off** the sugar mice.
run over (phr v)	/ˌrʌn ˈəʊvə(r)/	überfahren	The cars **ran over** the sugar mice.
troop into (phr v)	/ˈtruːp ˌɪntə/	strömen in	Hornby and his friends would **troop into** the sweet shop before every match.
build (v)	/bɪld/	zunehmen	The atmosphere at Chelsea games starts **building** 3 hours before kick-off.
draw (v)	/drɔː/	spielen	Arsenal **drew** 1-1 with Chelsea.
equalize (v)	/ˈiːkwəlaɪz/	ausgleichen	Sheringham **equalized** in the 89th minute.
exclude (v)	/ɪkˈskluːd/	ausschließen	He tried **excluding** friends who brought bad luck to the team.
set (v)	/set/	einstellen	I've **set** the video to record the match.
support (v)	/səˈpɔːt/	unterstützen	Which football team do you **support**?
tape (v)	/teɪp/	aufnehmen	Do you ever **tape** football matches?
tie (v)	/taɪ/	knoten	**Tie** a knot in your handkerchief as a reminder.
toss (v)	/tɒs/	werfen	They deliberately **tossed** the sugar mice into the road.
computer mad	/kəmpjuːtə ˈmæd/	verrückt nach Computern	Kids nowadays are **computer mad.**
get started on sth	/ɡet ˈstaːtɪd ɒn sʌmθɪŋ/	anfangen mit	You better **get started on your homework**.
10 minutes to go	/ˌten mɪnɪts tə ˈɡəʊ/	noch 10 Minuten dauern	With only **10 minutes to go**, I thought they'd lost the match.
Magic!	/ˈmædʒɪk/	Zauberei!	If I set the video I can watch the whole match again. **Magic**!
nothing but trouble	/nʌθɪŋ bət ˈtrʌbl/	nichts als Ärger	He tried to exclude friends who he thought brought **nothing but trouble** for the team.
be one of the lads	/ˌwʌn əv ðə ˈlædz/	dazu gehören	Mark wasn't really interested in football – he just wanted to be **one of the lads**.
You know how it is.	/jə ˌnəʊ haʊ ɪt ˈɪz/	Du weißt schon.	I just wanted to be one of the lads, **you know how it is**.

Anniversary night out/A man and his car (p. 46–48)

boiling (adj)	/ˈbɔɪlɪŋ/	kochend heiß	The office is either **boiling** or freezing!
choking (adj)	/ˈtʃəʊkɪŋ/	nach Atem ringend	Dad always ends up with a carful of **choking** passengers.
cosy (adj)	/ˈkəʊzi/	behaglich	He puts a **cosy** blanket over the car.
freezing (adj)	/ˈfriːzɪŋ/	eiskalt	With the windows open, the office is **freezing**.
hair-raising (adj)	/ˈheəreɪzɪŋ/	schauerlich	I hate people who drive at **hair-raising** speed.
half-finished (adj)	/ˌhaːfˈfɪnɪʃt/	halb ausgetrunken	I wish she wouldn't leave **half-finished** cups of coffee on the desk.
repulsive (adj) (TS)	/rɪˈpʌlsɪv/	widerlich	The engine pumps out **repulsive** fumes.
ritualistic (adj) (TS)	/rɪtʃʊːəˈlɪstɪk/	gemäß Ritualen lebend	Dad is the most **ritualistic** person I know.
accidentally (adv) (TS)	/ˌæksɪˈdentlɪ/	aus Versehen	He worries we might **accidentally** brush against the car.
forever (adv)	/fə(r)ˈevə(r)/	fortwährend	She's **forever** talking to her boyfriend on the phone.

otherwise (adv)	/'ʌðəwaɪz/	sonst	He'd better stop looking at that waitress. **Otherwise** I'm going home.
affection (n) (TS)	/ə'fekʃn/	Zuneigung	Our car gets more **affection** than a pet would!
blanket (n)	/'blæŋkɪt/	Decke	Dad puts the car under a cosy **blanket**.
break (n)	/breɪk/	Pause	I think we both deserve a **break**.
carful (n) (TS)	/'ka:fl/	ein vollbesetztes Auto	The fumes mean Dad ends up with a **carful** of choking passengers.
crew (n) (TS)	/kru:/	Mannschaft	Perhaps Dad had a **crew** in the air force who let him get away with it.
date (n)	/deɪt/	Verabredung	Chris brought Shirley to the restaurant for their first **date**.
drive (n)	/draɪv/	Auffahrt	Dad reverses out of the **drive** at hair-raising speed.
fumes (n pl) (TS)	/fju:mz/	Abgase	Repulsive **fumes** fill the air.
handbrake (n) (TS)	/'hændbreɪk/	Handbremse	Don't forget to put the **handbrake** on when you park.
shake (n) (TS)	/ʃeɪk/	Schütteln	Dad always gives the box of matches a **shake**.
take-off (n) (TS)	/'teɪkɒf/	Abfahrt	Perhaps Dad indulged in this kind of ritual before **take-off**.
visibility (n) (TS)	/ˌvɪzə'bɪləti/	Sicht	All the smoke in the car reduces **visibility**.
brush against (phr v) (TS)	/'brʌʃ əgenst/	streifen	He worries they might **brush against** the car and damage it.
get away with (phr v)	/get ə'weɪ wɪð/	mit etwas davonkommen	Perhaps Dad's crew let him **get away with** it.
go on about (phr v)	/gəʊ ˌɒn əbaʊt/	weiterreden über	She will **go on about** her personal problems.
go through (phr v)	/gəʊ 'θru:/	durchmachen	We **go through** the same routine each morning.
indulge in (phr v) (TS)	/ɪn'dʌldʒ ɪn/	sich etwas erlauben	He probably used to **indulge in** this kind of ritual when he was in the air force.
knock over (phr v)	/nɒk 'əʊvə(r)/	umstoßen	If you leave those cups lying around someone will **knock** them **over**.
pat down (phr v) (TS)	/pæt 'daʊn/	flach klopfen	He spends a minute or two **patting** the tobacco **down**.
pump out (phr v) (TS)	/ˌpʌmp 'aʊt/	ausstoßen	The engine **pumps out** repulsive fumes into the fresh country air.
tap out (phr v) (TS)	/ˌtæp 'aʊt/	ausklopfen	He **taps out** any remaining tobacco.
tuck up (phr v)	/ˌtʌk 'ʌp/	zudecken	I like listening to stormy weather when I'm safely **tucked up** in bed.
bang (v)	/bæŋ/	schlagen	He doesn't like us **banging** the car doors shut.
charge (v)	/tʃa:dʒ/	berechnen	I feel like her therapist – I should **charge** her for my time.
involve (v) (TS)	/ɪn'vɒlv/	betreffen	Most of his rituals **involve** his car.
puff (v) (TS)	/pʌf/	paffen	Stop **puffing** that pipe!
resent (v)	/rɪ'zent/	sich an etwas stören	I **resent** her telling me what to do.
reverse (v)	/rɪ'vɜ˞s/	rückwärts fahren	He always **reverses** out of the drive at high speed.
run (v) (TS)	/rʌn/	fahren	The buses aren't **running** today.
stuff (v) (TS)	/stʌf/	stopfen	He **stuffs** tobacco into the bowl of his pipe.
take (v) (TS)	/teɪk/	Feuer fangen	The tobacco doesn't always **take** first go.
turn (v) (TS)	/tɜ:n/	laufen (Motor)	We sit there for 5 minutes with the engine **turning**.
vandalise (v) (TS)	/'vændəlaɪz/	mutwillig beschädigen	He must think we're going to **vandalise** the seats with our school shoes.
vary (v)	/'veəri/	variieren	My routine **varies** from day to day.
be up to sth	/bi: 'ʌp tə sʌmθɪŋ/	etwas tun	What time I get up depends on what I've **been up to** the night before!
blow kisses	/ˌbləʊ 'kɪsɪz/	einen Kuss zuwerfen	I'm tired of listening to her **blowing kisses** to her boyfriend over the phone.

can't help doing	/ˌkɑːnt help ˈduːɪŋ/	nicht anders können, als	Chris **couldn't help telling** Shirley he loved her.
(at) full blast	/(ət) ˌfʊl ˈblæst/	volle Kraft	Why do we have to have the heating on **at full blast**?
get on sb's nerves	/ˌget ɒn sʌmbɒdɪz ˈnɜːvz/	jmd. auf die Nerven gehen	She really **gets on my nerves** at times!
leave it/things till the last minute	/ˌliːv ɪt/θɪŋz tɪl ðə ˌlɑːst ˈmɪnɪt/	etwas auf die letzte Minute verschieben	Mum always **leaves things till the last minute**.
take one's time	/ˌteɪk wʌnz ˈtaɪm/	sich Zeit nehmen	She likes to **take her time** in the morning.
untold damage (TS)	/ˌʌntəʊld ˈdæmɪdʒ/	unermeßlicher Schaden	He thinks we might cause **untold damage** to his precious car.
who knows what (TS)	/ˌhuː ˌnəʊz ˈwɒt/	wer weiß was	They might cause **who knows what** damage to the car.

The big day (p. 49)

aisle (n)	/aɪl/	Mittelgang	At the end of the ceremony the bride and groom walk down the **aisle** together.
best man (n)	/ˌbest ˈmæn/	Zeremonienmeister	The **best man** helps the groom on his wedding day.
bride (n)	/braɪd/	Braut	What does the **bride** usually wear in your country?
bridesmaid (n)	/ˈbraɪdzmeɪd/	Brautjungfer	The **bridesmaids** help the bride on her wedding day.
coin (n)	/kɔɪn/	Münze	In Spain the groom puts 13 gold **coins** in the bride's hands.
evil spirits (n pl) (TS)	/ˌiːvl ˈspɪrɪts/	böse Geister	Someone holds a black umbrella over the bride's head to protect her from **evil spirits**.
groom (n)	/gruːm/	Bräutigam	Are there any special rituals concerning the **groom** in your country?
page boy (n)	/ˈpeɪdʒ ˌbɔɪ/	Junge, der bei der Hochzeitszeremonie assistiert	In some countries a **page boy** follows the bride up the aisle.
reception (n)	/rɪˈsepʃn/	Empfang	After the church ceremony there is usually a **reception**.
veil (n)	/veɪl/	Schleier	The bride's face is often covered by a **veil**.
witness (n)	/ˈwɪtnəs/	Zeuge	A **witness** has to sign the marriage certificate.
worldly goods (n pl) (TS)	/ˌwɜːldlɪ ˈgʊdz/	weltliche Güter	The coins symbolise the **worldly goods** they are going to receive.
pin (v)	/pɪn/	anheften	Guests **pin** money on the bride's and groom's clothes.

Small talk (p. 51)

Give my regards to ...	/ˌgɪv maɪ rɪˈgɑːdz tə/	Grüße .... von mir.	**Give my regards to** your family.
I'd better be going.	/aɪd ˌbetə bɪ ˈgəʊɪŋ/	Es ist besser, wenn ich gehe.	It's getting late. **I'd better be going**.
I'll be off.	/ˌaɪl bɪ ˈɒf/	Ich gehe.	**'I'll be off** then.' 'OK then, bye.'
Long time no see. (TS)	/ˌlɒŋ ˌtaɪm nəʊ ˈsiː/	Lange nicht gesehen.	**'Long time no see.'** 'Yes, it must be over a year.'
Look after oneself.	/ˌlʊk ˌɑːftə wʌnself/	Pass auf dich auf.	'Bye, Bob.' 'Bye, Ann, **look after yourself**.'
Missing you already.	/ˌmɪsɪŋ juː ɔːlˈredɪ/	Du fehlst mir schon jetzt.	'Love you.' **'Missing you already**.'
Take it easy. (Am E)	/ˌteɪk ɪt ˈiːzɪ/	Nimm's leicht.	**'Take it easy,** then.' 'And you.'
Thank you for having me.	/ˌθæŋk juː fə ˈhævɪŋ mɪ/	Danke für die Gastfreundschaft.	I've had a lovely time. **Thank you for having me**.

Unit 6

Text messaging/Online (p. 52–55)

addicted (adj)	/əˈdɪktɪd/	süchtig	Some people are **addicted** to computer games.
entitled (adj)	/ɪnˈtaɪtld/	betitelt	The magazine was **entitled** '24 hours on the Net'.
flirtatious (adj)	/flɜːˈteɪʃəs/	kokett	I had a very **flirtatious** online conversation with someone aged 50.
glorified (adj)	/ˈglɔːrɪfaɪd/	glorifiziert	In my opinion, computers are just **glorified** hairdryers or electric kettles.
jet black (adj)	/ˌdʒet ˈblæk/	pechschwarz	It's a huge **jet black** computer.
work-related (adj)	/ˌwɜːkrɪˈleɪtəd/	mit Arbeit zu tun habend	Only 10% of text messages are **work-related**.
access (n)	/ˈækses/	Zugang	Does your mobile phone have Internet **access**?
characters (n pl)	/ˈkærəktəz/	Zeichen	You can send text messages of 160 **characters** for less than the price of a phone call.
geek (n)	/giːk/	Besessener	A **geek** is someone who is obsessed with computers.
juicer (n)	/ˈdʒuːsə(r)/	Entsafter	I use the **juicer** for making milk shakes.
row (n)	/raʊ/	Streit	In a recent survey 53% of people said they used text-messaging to apologise after **row**s.
screen (n)	/skriːn/	Bildschirm	You should take regular breaks when working on a computer **screen**.
survey (n)	/ˈsɜːveɪ/	Meinungsumfrage	We decided to do a **survey** of mobile-phone users.
text-messaging (n)	/ˈtekstˌmesɪdʒɪŋ/	Textnachrichten versenden	What are the advantages of **text-messaging**?
user (n)	/ˈjuːzə(r)/	Benutzer	What percentage of the population are mobile-phone **users**?
vending machine (n)	/ˈvendɪŋ məʃiːn/	Automat (um etwas zu verkaufen)	In some places you can send a text message to a **vending machine**!
turn out (phr v)	/ˌtɜːn ˈaʊt/	sich erweisen	The person I was e-mailing **turned out** to be fifteen.
cut and paste	/ˌkʌt ən ˈpeɪst/	ausschneiden und einfügen	**Cut and paste** is one of the functions I use most frequently.
get a life	/ˌget ə ˈlaɪf/	ein normales Leben führen	You should **get a life** instead of spending all your time playing computer games.
get stuck	/ˌget ˈstʌk/	sich aufhängen	I hate it when computer programs **get stuck.**
go wrong	/ˌgəʊ ˈrɒŋ/	verkehrt laufen	Computers are great until they **go wrong**!
It nearly killed me!	/ɪt ˌnɪəli ˈkɪld mi/	Es hätte mich fast ungebracht!	I once spent 24 hours on the Internet and **it nearly killed me**!
a love-hate relationship	/ə ˌlʌvheɪt rɪˈleɪʃnʃɪp/	Hassliebe	A lot of people have **a love-hate relationship** with computers.
of one sort or another	/əv ˌwʌn sɔːt ɔː(r) əˈnʌðə(r)/	den einen oder anderen	I've had a computer **of one sort or another** since 1987.
plain English	/ˌpleɪn ˈɪŋglɪʃ/	einfaches Deutsch	Why aren't computer manuals written in **plain English**?

20

Lara Croft (p. 56)

biggest-selling (adj)	/ˈbɪgəstˈselɪŋ/	meistgekauft	Tomb Raider is one of the world's **biggest-selling** video games.
challenging (adj) (TS)	/ˈtʃæləndʒɪŋ/	eine Herausforderung bietend	Lara likes extreme skiing and spent a holiday searching for **challenging** terrain.
crispy (adj) (TS)	/ˈkrɪspɪ/	knusprig	One of her favourite foods is **crispy** tarantula.
frosty (adj) (TS)	/ˈvfrɒstɪ/	zurückhaltend	Her parents are a bit **frosty** towards her.

honeyed (adj) (TS)	/'hʌnɪd/	mit Honig gesüßt	Another of her favourite foods is **honeyed** stick insects.
smoked (adj) (TS)	/sməʊkt/	geräuchert	She also likes **smoked** iguana.
unreasonable (adj) (TS)	/ʌn'riːznəbl/	unangemessen	Do you think the attitude of Lara's parents is **unreasonable**?
literally (adv) (TS)	/'lɪtərəlɪ/	wortwörtlich	I first got involved in the missions by accident – **literally**.
allowance (n) (TS)	/ə'laʊəns/	finanzielle Unterstützung	Lara's parents have stopped her **allowance**.
attic conversion (n)	/'ætɪk kən vɜːʒn/	umgebauter Dachboden	Does Lara live in an **attic conversion**?
estate (n) (TS)	/ɪ'steɪt/	Besitz	She hunts in the woods around her **estate**.
extreme sports (n pl)	/ɪk stri:m 'spɔ:ts/	extreme Sportarten	Have you ever taken part in **extreme sports**?
hunting (n)	/'hʌntɪŋ/	Jagen	She loves **hunting** in the woods.
mansion (n)	/'mænʃn/	Herrenhaus	A **mansion** is a large house, often in the countryside.
needlework (n)	/'niːdlwɜːk/	Näharbeit	**Needlework** involves sewing things such as cushions.
perseverance (n) (TS)	/ˌpɜːsɪ'vɪərəns/	Durchhaltevermögen	I really admire his **perseverance**.
stick insects (n pl) (TS)	/'stɪk ɪnseks/	Stabinsekten	**Stick insects** are insects with long thin bodies.
survivor (n) (TS)	/sə'vaɪvə(r)/	Überlebende(r)	She was the only **survivor** of a plane crash in the Himalayas.
terrain (n) (TS)	/tə'reɪn/	Gebiet	She enjoys skiing over difficult **terrain**.
weapons (n pl)	/'wepənz/	Waffen	She spends all her money on **weapons**.
pop into (phr v) (TS)	/'pɒp ɪntə/	bei jmd. vorbeischauen	I use my Norton Streetfighter for **popping into** the village.
settle down (phr v)	/ˌsetl 'daʊn/	ein regelmäßiges Leben führen	Would you like to **settle down** and get married?
search (v) (TS)	/sɜːtʃ/	suchen	What are you **searching** for?
strap (v)	/stræp/	festbinden	Her dream is to ski down Mount Everest with Brian Blessed **strapped** to her back.
by accident (TS)	/baɪ 'æksɪdənt/	durch Zufall	She first got involved in the missions **by accident.**
ever since (TS)	/ˌevə 'sɪns/	seitdem	It happened after the accident and I've been going on missions **ever since**.
a fussy eater (TS)	/ə ˌfʌsɪ 'iːtə(r)/	ein schwieriger Esser	She's not **a fussy eater** – she's eaten iguana, tarantula and stick insects.
get a taste for sth (TS)	/ˌget ə 'teɪst fə sʌmθɪŋ/	Gefallen finden an	I **got a taste for adventure** after my plane went down in the Himalayas.
Good heavens. (TS)	/ˌgʊd 'hevnz/	Lieber Himmel.	**Good heavens**, Lara. You are an unusual person.
stand in one's way (TS)	/sʌmθɪŋ ˌstænd ɪn wɒnz 'weɪ/	im Wege stehen	I've succeeded because I've never let **anything stand in my way**.
'Mr Right'	/ˌmɪstə 'raɪt/	der Richtige	Would you like to meet **'Mr Right'** and settle down?
the way sb looks (TS)	/ðə ˌweɪ sʌmbədɪ 'lʊks/	Aussehen	Do you think you've only been successful because of **the way you look**?

Has technology ruined childhood? (p. 59–61)

communal (adj)	/kə'mjuːnl/	gemeinsam	Younger children tend to play in **communal** spaces such as the sitting room or garden.
computer-literate (adj)	/kəmpjuːtə'lɪtrət/	computergewandt	Most teenagers nowadays are **computer-literate**.
inappropriate (adj)	/ˌɪnə'prəʊprɪət/	unangebracht	People use mobile phones in **inappropriate** places.
increasing (adj)	/ɪn'kriːsɪŋ/	zunehmend	**Increasing** prosperity has contributed to the rise of bedroom culture.
individualistic (adj)	/ˌɪndɪvɪdʒʊə'lɪstɪk/	individualistisch	Children spend a lot of time doing **individualistic** activities.
interactive (adj) (TS)	/ˌɪntər'æktɪv/	interaktiv	I prefer computer games to TV because they're **interactive**.

offending (adj)	/əˈfendɪŋ/	irritierend	The **offending** mobile phones were banned from a pub in Oxford.
spacious (adj)	/ˈspeɪʃəs/	geräumig	Homes are more **spacious** than they used to be.
worrying (adj)	/ˈwʌriɪŋ/	besorgniserregend	Some children spend a **worrying** amount of time playing computer games or watching TV.
moreover (adv)	/mɔːrˈəʊvə(r)/	außerdem	**Moreover**, the distinction between individualistic use and social activities is less extreme than people think.
nevertheless (adv)	/ˌnevəðəˈles/	dennoch	**Nevertheless**, 57% of children say they still enjoy reading.
yet (conjunction)	/jet/	aber	**Yet**, if children had the chance, they would prefer to go out more.
air traffic control	/eə ˌtræfɪk kənˈtrəʊl/	Flugverkehrskontrolle	**Air traffic control** have banned the toys from all flights.
bedroom culture (n)	/ˈbedruːm ˌkʌltʃə(r)/	Schlafzimmerkultur	Several factors have contributed to the rise of **bedroom culture**.
book-lover (n)	/ˈbʊklʌvə(r)/	Bücherliebhaber	Many children said they were still **book-lover**s.
circuit board (n)	/ˈsɜːkɪt ˌbɔːd/	Platine	The problem was caused by a mouse leaving droppings on the **circuit board**!
disturbance (n)	/dɪˈstɜːbəns/	Störung	Mobile phones often cause a **disturbance** when they ring.
droppings (n pl)	/ˈdrɒpɪŋz/	Köttel	The problem was caused by mouse **droppings** on the circuit board.
Internet connection (n)	/ˌɪntənet kəˈnekʃn/	Internetanschluss	Do you have an **Internet connection** in your bedroom?
music installation (n)	/ˈmjuːzɪk ɪnstəˌleɪʃn/	Stereoanlage	68% of children have their own **music installation**.
prosperity (n)	/prɒˈsperɪ/	Wohlstand	Increasing **prosperity** means people are buying more and more gadgets.
single (n)	/ˈsɪŋgl/	Single	She bought a Beatles **single** but never played it!
'snail mail'	/ˈsneɪl ˌmeɪl/	herkömmliche Post	**'Snail mail'** means writing letters rather than sending e-mails.
soap character (n)	/ˈsəʊp ˌkærəktəz/	Figur aus eiener Soap	Children enjoy talking about **soap characters** .
social skills (n pl)	/ˈsəʊʃl ˌskɪlz/	soziale Fertigkeiten	It's important for children to develop **social skills**.
viewing (n)	/ˈvjuːɪŋ/	Schauen	Do you agree that too much TV **viewing** is bad for children?
class sb as sth (phr v)	/ˈklɑːs əz/	betrachten als	Only one child in a hundred could be **classed as an addict**.
go up (phr v)	/gəʊ ˈʌp/	nach oben gehen	My parents usually tell me to **go up** around 9.30.
stay up (phr v)	/steɪ ˈʌp/	aufbleiben	A lot of children **stay up** watching TV for as long as they wish.
devote (v)	/dɪˈvəʊt/	aufwenden	On average children **devote** five hours a day to screen media.
gossip (v)	/ˈgɒsɪp/	klatschen	Children enjoy **gossiping** about soap characters.
interact (v)	/ˌɪntərˈækt/	interagieren	They need to **interact** with each other.
proliferate (v)	/prəˈlɪfəreɪt/	sich vermehren	The use of PCs has **proliferated** in the past 5 years.
retreat (v)	/rɪˈtriːt/	sich zurückziehen	It's traditional for British teenagers to **retreat** to their bedrooms.
ruin (v)	/ˈruːɪn/	ruinieren	Has technology **ruined** childhood?
socialise (v)	/ˈsəʊʃəlaɪz/	sich unterhalten, sich treffen	Children now use their bedrooms as a place to **socialise**.
as a result	/æz ə rɪˈzʌlt/	demzufolge	Parents are worried about safety and **as a result** children spend more time indoors.
commonly assumed	/ˌkɒmənli əˈsjuːmd/	allgemein angenommen	The distinction between individualistic use and social activities is less extreme than is **commonly assumed**.
draw the line (at)	/drɔː ðə ˈlaɪn (ət)/	die Grenze ziehen	I **draw the line** at my kids going to bed after 10 pm.
even so	/ˈiːvn ˈsəʊ/	aber doch	Many children devote five hours a day to screen media; **even so** only one child in a hundred is a screen addict.

22

get far more out of sth (TS)	/get ˌfɑː mɔː ˈaʊt əv sʌmθɪŋ/	viel mehr davon haben	I **get far more out of reading a good book** than watching TV.
given the chance	/ˌgɪvn ðə ˈtʃaːns/	wenn ihnen die Möglichkeit geboten wird	**Given the chance**, children would rather go out than stay indoors.
be hooked up to sth	/bɪ ˌhʊkt ˈʌp tə sʌmθɪŋ/	verbunden sein mit	34% have a games controller **hooked up to the TV**.
in my case (TS)	/ɪn ˈmaɪ keɪs/	in meinem Fall	I like getting letters – even though it's usually a bill **in my case**!
have mixed feelings about (TS)	/hæv mɪks ˈfiːlɪŋz əbaʊt/	gemischte Gefühle haben bezüglich	I **have mixed feelings about** the Internet.
kill time	/ˌkɪl ˈtaɪm/	die Zeit totschlagen	A lot of people use TV as a way of **killing time**.
lose oneself in	/ˈluːz wʌnself ɪn/	sich selber verlieren in	Children can **lose themselves in** activities such as TV viewing and computer games.
make contact with	/meɪk ˈkɒntækt wɪð/	Kontakt knüpfen mit	They like to use the Internet to **make contact with** other kids.
on average	/ɒn ˈævərɪdʒ/	durchschnittlich	**On average** children devote five hours a day to screen media.
shut oneself away	/ʃʌt wʌnself əˈweɪ/	sich absondern	Children are now **shutting themselves away** in their bedrooms with a TV or computer.
There's a limit to … (TS)	/ðeəz ə ˈlɪmɪt tə/	Alles hat seine Grenzen.	**There's a limit to** how long you can sit in front of a screen.

Unit 7

Review (p. 62–67)

chauffeur-driven (adj)	/ˈʃəʊfəˌdrɪvn/	chauffiert	Gunther tours the countryside in a **chauffeur-driven** Mercedes.
fake (adj)	/feɪk/	falsch	Hughes used to scatter **fake** jewels on the pavement.
former (adj)	/ˈfɔːmə(r)/	ehemalig	Gunther bought Madonna's **former** home.
pioneering (adj)	/ˌpaɪəˈnɪərɪŋ/	Pionierarbeit leistend	Howard Hughes was a **pioneering** aviator and industrialist.
ready-prepared (adj)	/ˌredɪprɪˈpeəd/	Fertig-	Do you ever buy **ready-prepared** salad?
slimy (adj)	/ˈslaɪmɪ/	schleimig	She felt something large and **slimy** in the bag of salad.
sound-proofed (adj)	/ˈsaʊndpruːft/	schalldicht	The studio is **sound-proofed** so you can't hear any noise.
startled (adj)	/ˈstɑːtld/	erschrocken	James West used to throw silver dollars to **startled** onlookers from his car.
acutely (adv)	/əˈkjuːtlɪ/	ernstlich	He was **acutely** nervous of the outside world.
agony aunt (n)	/ˈægənɪ ˌɑːnt/	Kummerkastentante	An **agony aunt** is someone who answers people's problems in magazines.
chat room (n)	/ˈtʃæt ˌruːm/	Chatroom	Have you ever visited an Internet **chat room**?
dip (n)	/dɪp/	Sprung	Do you fancy a **dip** in the swimming pool?
dust (n)	/dʌst/	Staub	**Dust** covered the surface of every table and chair in the room.
highway (n) (Am E)	/ˈhaɪweɪ/	Autobahn	He used to race along the Texas **highway**s.
meanness (n)	/ˈmiːnəs/	Geiz	John Paul Getty was famous for his **meanness**.
newspaper publishing (n)	/ˈnjuːspeɪpə ˌpʌblɪʃɪŋ/	Verlegen von Zeitungen	Pulitzer was a **newspaper publishing** magnate.
onlooker (n)	/ˈɒnlʊkə(r)/	Zuschauer	Startled **onlooker**s watched as he threw them handfuls of silver dollars.
ordeal (n)	/ɔːˈdiːl/	Tortur	Mrs Henderson is still recovering from her **ordeal**.
paw print (n)	/ˈpɔː ˌprɪnt/	Pfotenabdruck	There were **paw print**s all over the carpet.

pay phone (n)	/'peɪ ˌfəʊn/	Münztelefon	He used to make his guests use a **pay phone** in the hall.
property (n)	/'prɒpətɪ/	Immobilien	Gunther also owns **property** in Germany.
purchase (n)	/'pɜːtʃəs/	Ankauf	He's currently thinking about his next **purchase**.
spokesperson (n)	/'spəʊkspɜːsn/	Sprecher(in)	A **spokesperson** for the supermarket said they had no idea how the snake got into the bag.
tycoon (n)	/taɪˈkuːn/	Magnat	Brian Hughes was a well-known manufacturing **tycoon**.
give in (to) (phr v)	/gɪv ˈɪn (tə)/	nachgeben	Everyone **gives in to** temptation from time to time.
go off (phr v)	/ˌgəʊ ˈɒf/	sauer werden	Ugh! The milk's **gone off**.
go on (phr v)	/ˌgəʊ ˈɒn/	fortfahren / sich abspielen	(Sense 1) We all **go on** getting older. / (Sense 2) Is something **going on** between those two?
put off (phr v)	/ˌpʊt ˈɒf/	aufschieben	Don't keep **putting** things **off**.
scheme up (phr v)	/ˌskiːm ˈʌp/	aushecken	Does Madonna enjoy **scheming up** new images?
speed by (phr v)	/ˌspiːd ˈbaɪ/	vorbeirasen	Cars kept overtaking and **speeding by** us.
postpone (v)	/pəʊsˈpəʊn/	verschieben	The match had to be **postponed** because of rain.
reject (v)	/rɪˈdʒekt/	abweisen	Gunther had earlier **rejected** Stallone's $25 million estate.
scatter (v)	/'skætə(r)/	verstreuen	Hughes would **scatter** fake jewels on the pavement.
slither (v)	/'slɪðə(r)/	gleiten	The snake **slithered** across the kitchen table.
stare (v)	/steə(r)/	starren	The snake just **stared** at her.
submit (to) (v)	/səbˈmɪt (tə)/	nachgeben	Oscar Wilde said that you should **submit** to temptation.
trade (v)	/treɪd/	(ein)tauschen	Madonna was asked if she had **traded** love for fame.
a grown woman	/ə ˌgrəʊn ˈwʊmən/	eine erwachsene Frau	**A grown woman** sucking her thumb! I don't believe it!
have a good nose for a bargain	/ˌhæv ə ɡʊd ˌnəʊz fə(r) ə ˈbɑːɡɪn/	ein feines Gespür für Schnäppchen haben	Some people have **a** really **good nose for a bargain**.
make oneself at home	/ˌmeɪk wʌnself ət ˈhəʊm/	sich wie zuhause fühlen	He's already **made himself** very much **at home** in Miami.
sign on the dotted line	/ˌsaɪn ɒn ðə ˌdɒtɪd ˈlaɪn/	unterschreiben Sie auf der gepunkteten Linie	Just **sign on the dotted line** and the house is yours.
suck one's thumb	/ˌsʌk wʌnz ˈθʌm/	Daumen lutschen	It's childish to **suck your thumb**.
the trouble with ...	/ðə ˈtrʌbl wɪð/	das Problem mit	Quentin Crisp said that **the trouble with** children is that you can't give them back.
this and that	/ˌðɪs ən ˈðæt/	dies und jenes	'What have you been doing recently?' 'Oh, you know, **this and that**.'
whatever you do	/wɒtˌevə jə ˈduː/	was auch Immer du tust	**Whatever you do**, don't lose your temper.

24

Unit 8

Escape/A day at the seaside (p. 68–70)

demanding (adj)	/dɪˈmɑːndɪŋ/	anspruchsvoll	The author's son is very **demanding**.
disturbing (adj)	/dɪˈstɜːbɪŋ/	störend	People find it **disturbing** when I take my shirt off in public.
half-eaten (adj)	/hɑːˈfiːtn/	halb aufgegessen	He started to nibble a **half-eaten** sandwich.
heartbreaking (adj)	/'hɑːtbreɪkɪŋ/	herzzerreißend	The **heartbreaking** thing is, she really means it.

inflatable (adj)	/ɪnˈfleɪtəbl/	aufblasbar	They went out on the sea in an **inflatable** dinghy.
playful (adj)	/ˈpleɪfl/	spielerisch	His wife gave him a **playful** slap.
preposterous (adj)	/prɪˈpɒstərəs/	lächerlich	She was wearing a **preposterous** sunhat.
sharp (adj)	/ʃɑːp/	scharf	The children spent the time poking each other with **sharp** objects.
sunburned (adj)	/ˈsʌnbɜːnd/	von der Sonne verbrannt	We got terribly **sunburned**.
windburned (adj)	/ˈwɪndbɜːnd/	vom Wind verbrannt	It's easy to get **windburned** without noticing it.
casually (adv)	/ˈkæʒuəli/	nebenbei	His daughter **casually** mentioned that the dog had had a bite from the sandwich.
frankly (adv)	/ˈfræŋklɪ/	ehrlich gesagt	**Frankly**, I don't understand why the British love the seaside so much.
gaily (adv)	/ˈɡeɪlɪ/	fröhlich	'Oh, look, he's eating the sandwich left by the dog,' she said **gaily**.
serenely (adv)	/səˈriːnlɪ/	ruhig	'You'll have to take him to Kennebunkport,' she said **serenely**.
soothingly (adv)	/ˈsuːðɪŋlɪ/	beruhigend	'Don't worry,' she said **soothingly**.
warily (adv)	/ˈweərəlɪ/	vorsichtig	'What do you want to go to the beach for?' he said **warily**.
attachment (n)	/əˈtætʃmənt/	Zuneigung	I don't understand the British **attachment** to the seaside.
candy floss (n)	/ˈkændɪ ˌflɒs/	Zuckerwatte	**Candy floss** is a sugary sweet like cotton wool that you eat on a stick.
convention (n)	/kənˈvenʃn/	Konferenz	There's a trade **convention** in Birmingham next week.
dinghy (n)	/ˈdɪŋɪ/	(Schlauch)boot	We hired an inflatable **dinghy**.
exhibit (n)	/ɪɡˈzɪbɪt/	Ausstellungsstück	I was so sunburned that I felt like an **exhibit** at a convention.
paddle (n)	/ˈpædl/	Paddelfahrt	Children enjoy going for a **paddle** in the sea.
prospect (n)	/ˈprɒspekt/	Aussicht	How does he feel about the **prospect** of a day on the beach?
saltwater (n)	/ˈsɒltwɔːtə(r)/	Salzwasser	My wife is English and is therefore obsessed with **saltwater**.
seaside (n)	/ˈsiːsaɪd/	Küste	Do you like going to the **seaside**?
slap (n)	/slæp/	Klaps	His wife gave him a playful **slap**.
surf (n)	/sɜːf/	Brandung	I watched them slowly emerging from the **surf**.
tar (n)	/tɑː(r)/	Teer	One of his daughters got **tar** in her hair.
water slide (n)	/ˈwɔːtə ˌslaɪd/	Wasserrutschbahn	My son told me he needed his own **water slide**.
set off (phr v)	/ˌset ˈɒf/	abfahren	What time did you **set off** home?
bury (v)	/ˈberɪ/	eingraben	His son was **burying** him in sand.
chuckle (v)	/ˈtʃʌkl/	kichern	What are you **chuckling** about?
emerge (v)	/ɪˈmɜːdʒ/	zum Vorschein kommen	I watched as they **emerged** from the surf.
nip (v)	/nɪp/	leicht beißen	The dog **nipped** me on the leg.
reassure (v)	/ˌriːəˈʃʊə(r)/	versichern	My wife **reassured** me that we'd have a great time.
whimper (v)	/ˈwɪmpə(r)/	jammern	'Oh, no,' he **whimpered**.
beyond the reach of	/bɪjɒnd ðə ˈriːtʃ əv/	außer Reichweite	My wife is **beyond the reach of** reason where saltwater is concerned.
get one's own way	/ˌɡet wʌnz əʊn ˈweɪ/	seinen Willen bekommen	Do you usually **get your own way**?
put one's foot down	/ˌpʊt wʌnz ˈfʊt daʊn/	energisch auftreten	Sometimes you have to **put your foot down** and say 'no'.
survey the scene	/səˌveɪ ðə ˈsiːn/	die Situation in Augenschein nehmen	He quickly **surveyed the scene** and told me what he would need.

Where's my car? (p. 71)

extravagant (adj)	/ɪkˈstrævəgənt/	extravagant	He used the money to splash out on an **extravagant** holiday.
five-star (adj)	/ˈfaɪvstɑː(r)/	Fünf-Sterne-	He booked a suite in a **five-star** hotel.
previously (adv)	/ˈpriːvɪəslɪ/	zuvor	He told his girlfriend he had inherited the money a few months **previously**.
community service (n)	/kəˌmjuːnətɪ ˈsɜːvɪs/	Dienstleistung	The court ordered him to do six-months' **community service**.
con-man (n)	/ˈkɒnmæn/	Betrüger	A **con-man** is someone who deceives people in order to get money.
theft (n)	/θeft/	Diebstahl	Townsend was charged with **theft**.
charge (v)	/tʃɑːdʒ/	beschuldigen	They **charged** him with theft.
prosecute (v)	/ˈprɒsɪkjuːt/	(gerichtlich) verfolgen	It was a difficult decision for Mrs Hawkin to **prosecute** her own son.
serve (v)	/sɜːv/	ableisten	He is now **serving** six-months' community service.
appear in court	/əˈpɪə(r) ɪn ˈkɔːt/	vor Gericht erscheinen	The teenager **appeared in court**, charged with theft.
be registered in sb's name	/bɪ ˌredʒɪstəd ɪn sʌmbədɪz ˈneɪm/	unter dem Namen von jmd. eingetragen sein	The car **was registered in his mother's name**.
show concern	/ʃəʊ kənˈsɜːn/	Besorgnis bekunden	He had a strange way of **showing concern**.
a string of lies	/ə ˌstrɪŋ əv ˈlaɪz/	eine Menge Lügen	He told his girlfriend **a string of lies**.
without sb's knowledge	/wɪˌðaʊt sʌmbədɪz ˈnɒlɪdʒ/	ohne jmd. Mitwissen	The car was sold **without her knowledge**.

I'll never forget you (p. 72–73)

extraordinary (adj) (TS)	/ɪkˈstrɔːdnrɪ/	außergewöhnlich	Anything ordinary felt **extraordinary** because we were together.
inseparable (adj) (TS)	/ɪnˈseprəbl/	unzertrennlich	Gill and Tony eventually became **inseparable**.
mutual (adj) (TS)	/ˈmjuːtʃʊəl/	gegenseitig	Angela and Brad met through a **mutual** friend.
real-life (adj) (TS)	/ˌrɪəlˈlaɪf/	alltäglich	Our relationship wasn't strong enough for **real-life** problems.
actually (adv)	/ˈæktʃʊəlɪ/	tatsächlich	'Have you ever had a holiday romance?' 'I have **actually**.'
bliss (n) (TS)	/blɪs/	Glückseligkeit	At the beginning it was **bliss**.
immigration officer (n)	/ˌɪmɪˈgreɪʃn ˌɒfɪsə(r)/	Beamter für Einwanderungsangelegenheiten	Why did **immigration officer**s hold Brad in London?
soulmate (n) (TS)	/ˈsəʊlmeɪt/	Busenfreund	Angela thought she had met her **soulmate**.
hold up (phr v) (TS)	/ˌhəʊld ˈʌp/	aufhalten	I wondered what was **holding** him **up**.
sort out (phr v)	/ˌsɔːt ˈaʊt/	klären	We both had other relationships to **sort out**.
step in (phr v) (TS)	/ˌstep ˈɪn/	sich einmischen	A friend **stepped in** and arranged our first date.
deport (v) (TS)	/dɪˈpɔːt/	ausweisen	Eventually Brad was **deported** back to Australia.
hold (v)	/həʊld/	festhalten	Why was Brad **held** by immigration officers?
resist (v)	/rɪˈzɪst/	widerstehen	Tony **resisted** her at first.
surrender (v)	/səˈrendə(r)/	sich ergeben	In the end he **surrendered**.

Do you know what I mean?	/ju nəʊ wɒt aɪ miːn/	Kapierst du, was ich meine?	I thought, 'He's the one for me.' **Do you know what I mean?**
be the type to do sth	/bi ðə ˌtaɪp tə 'duː sʌmθɪŋ/	der Typ sein, etwas zu tun	I didn't think you were **the type to have a holiday romance.**
come to think of it	/kʌm tə 'θɪŋk əv ɪt/	wenn ich darüber nachdenke	**Come to think of it,** he did look a little like Brad Pitt.
(fall) head over heels (in love) (TS)	/fɔːl ˌhed əʊvə ˌhiːlz (ɪnlʌv)/	(sich) Hals über Kopf (verlieben)	While Angela was in Sydney she **fell head over heels in love.**
it was over (TS)	/ɪt wəz 'əʊvə(r)/	es war vorbei	For me at least, **it was over.**
It (all) worked out well in the end.	/ɪt (ɔːl) wɜːkt aʊt ˌwel ɪn ðiː'end/	Ende gut, alles gut.	We ended up getting married so **it all worked out well in the end.**
to be more precise	/tə bi ˌmɔː prɪ'saɪs/	um genau zu sein	I went travelling in Australia, well Sydney, **to be more precise.**
to put it simply	/tə ˌpʊt ɪt 'sɪmplɪ/	einfach gesagt	It wasn't the best of beginnings, **to put it simply.**
worship sb from afar (TS)	/ˌwɜːʃɪp sʌmbədɪ frəm ə'fɑː(r)/	jmd. aus der Ferne anhimmeln	At first I just **worshipped him from afar.**

Every postcard tells a story/Never again!/Insider's guide (p. 74–76)

arty (adj)	/'ɑːtɪ/	kunstsinnig, Künstler-	An **arty** person is interested in art and culture.
bookish (adj)	/'bʊkɪʃ/	Bücherwurm, Leseratte	A **bookish** person reads a lot.
caring (adj)	/'keərɪŋ/	fürsorglich	Rob's a kind **caring** person.
crisp (adj)	/krɪsp/	frisch	Enjoy the **crisp** mountain air!
dazzling (adj)	/'dæzlɪŋ/	strahlend	The weather was sunny with **dazzling** skies.
devilish (adj)	/'devəlɪʃ/	teuflisch	Kids sometimes behave in the most **devilish** way.
disobedient (adj)	/ˌdɪsə'biːdɪənt/	ungehorsam	They're often **disobedient**.
endless (adj)	/'endləs/	unendlich (viele)	They have **endless** competitions to see who can behave the worst.
exhilarating (adj)	/ɪg'zɪləreɪtɪŋ/	aufregend	Madrid is an **exhilarating** city.
happy-go-lucky (adj)	/ˌhæpɪgəʊ'lʌkɪ/	sorglos	Would you describe yourself as a **happy-go-lucky** sort of person?
illegible (adj)	/ɪ'ledʒəbl/	unleserlich	Her handwriting is **illegible**.
image-conscious (adj)	/'ɪmɪdʒˌkɒnʃəs/	auf sein Image achtend	Arty people can be very **image-conscious**.
indecisive (adj)	/ˌɪndɪ'saɪsɪv/	unentschlossen	**Indecisive** people often try to please everyone.
long-winded (adj)	/ˌlɒŋ'wɪndəd/	weitschweifig	**Long-winded** descriptions can be very boring.
relentless (adj)	/rɪ'lentləs/	unerbittlich	When the children are awake, they're **relentless**.
saucy (adj)	/'sɔːsɪ/	schlüpfrig	A **saucy** postcard is funny in a way that is slightly rude.
scrawny (adj)	/'skrɔːnɪ/	spindeldürr	Someone who is **scrawny** is very thin.
sickly (adj)	/'sɪklɪ/	unangenehm süß	**Sickly** food is sweet and sugary.
stark-naked (adj)	/ˌstɑːk'neɪkɪd/	splitternackt	The weather girls or boys appear on the screen **stark-naked**.
stylish (adj)	/'staɪlɪʃ/	stilvoll	She always wears very **stylish** clothes.
tacky (adj)	/'tækɪ/	billig, geschmacklos	A **tacky** postcard is not very stylish but is often amusing.
tasteful (adj)	/'teɪstfl/	geschmackvoll	Arty people tend to send **tasteful** postcards.
tasteless (adj)	/'teɪstləs/	geschmacklos	Have you ever sent a tacky **tasteless** postcard?
tearful (adj)	/'tɪəfl/	weinerlich	She arrived at her parents' house feeling **tearful**.
time-conscious (adj)	/'taɪmˌkɒnʃəs/	zeitbewusst	People nowadays are increasingly **time-conscious**.

unadventurous (adj)	/ˌʌnəd'ventʃərəs/	nicht abenteuerlich	Don't be so **unadventurous**!
unselfconscious (adj)	/ˌʌnself'kɒnʃəs/	ungezwungen	He's an **unselfconscious** person who enjoys life.
unwilling (adj)	/ʌn'wɪlɪŋ/	widerwillig	She's **unwilling** to travel with three children now.
well-informed (adj)	/ˌwelɪn'fɔːmd/	gut informiert	Someone who is **well-informed** about a subject knows a lot about it.
well-poured (adj)	/wel'pɔːd/	gut eingeschenkt	There's nothing better than a **well-poured** Guinness!
accordingly (adv)	/ə'kɔːdɪŋlɪ/	dementsprechend	The next day's temperature appears on the screen and the weather girl or boy dresses **accordingly**.
individually (adv)	/ˌɪndɪ'vɪdʒʊəlɪ/	einzeln	**Individually,** they're easier to deal with than all together.
angle (n)	/'æŋgl/	Blickwinkel	The weather forecast is presented from an interesting new **angle**.
bagful (n)	/'bægfʊl/	Tasche voll	She took a **bagful** of toys for the journey.
bulletin (n)	/'bʊlətɪn/	Bulletin	I missed the late-night news **bulletin**.
culture vulture (n)	/'kʌltʃə ˌvʌltʃə(r)/	Kulturliebhaber	Sight-seeing is a way of life for the **culture vulture**.
goo (n)	/guː/	klebriger Brei	A **goo** is a messy substance like a thick liquid.
joker (n)	/'dʒəʊkə(r)/	Witzbold	A **joker** is someone who enjoys laughing and having fun.
parking permit (n)	/'pɑːkɪŋ ˌpɜːmɪt/	Parkerlaubnis	You need a **parking permit** to park here.
parking restrictions (n pl)	/'pɑːkɪŋ rɪˌstrɪkʃənz/	Parkregeln	**Parking restrictions** apply throughout the city.
pocketful (n)	/'pɒkɪtfʊl/	Tasche voll	She took a **pocketful** of sweets with her for the journey.
ribtickler (n)	/'rɪbˌtɪklə(r)/	guter Witz	A **ribtickler** is an informal word for something that is very funny.
saying (n)	/'seɪɪŋ/	Redensart	A **saying** is a sentence or phrase that is very well known.
back on to (phr v)	/'bæk ɒn tə/	grenzen an	The beaches **back on to** the national park.
soak up (phr v)	/ˌsəʊk 'ʌp/	annehmen	Do you enjoy **soaking up** the local culture when you're on holiday?
reveal (v)	/rɪ'viːl/	offenbaren	Your choice of postcard **reveals** a lot about you.
be a handful	/'hændfʊl/	jmd. in Trab halten	The children can **be a** real **handful** at times.
be bound to	/bɪ 'baʊnd tə/	etw. sicher tun	Humorous postcards **are bound to** raise a smile.
don't be fooled	/ˌdəʊnt bɪ 'fuːld/	lass dich nicht täuschen	**Don't be fooled** by appearances.
downright irresponsible	/ˌdaʊnraɪt ˌɪrɪ'spɒnsəbl/	einfach verantwortungslos	The journey with three children wasn't just foolish – it was **downright irresponsible**.
The final straw was …	/ðə ˌfaɪnl 'strɔː wəz/	Der Tropfen, der das Fass zum Überlaufen brachte, war …	**The final straw was** when my parents told me what an awful child I had been.
go out of one's way to do sth	/gəʊ ˌaʊt əv wʌnz 'weɪ tə duː sʌmθɪŋ/	sein Bestes geben	Arty people **go out of their way to find** unusual postcards.
love the sound of one's own voice	/lʌv ðə ˌsaʊnd əv wʌnz əʊn 'vɔɪs/	sich gerne reden hören	People who write long-winded descriptions tend to be the type who **love the sound of their own voice**.
make the most of	/meɪk ðə 'məʊst əv/	das Beste aus etwas machen	It's important to **make the most of** your holiday.
be mistaken for	/bɪ mɪ'steɪkən fə(r)/	verwechselt werden mit	I would hate to **be mistaken for** one of the crowd.
more often than not	/mɔː 'ɒfn ðən 'nɒt/	in den meisten Fällen	**More often than not**, they're disobedient.
on top of that	/ɒn 'tɒp əv 'ðæt/	abgesehen davon	**On top of that**, they all want my attention at the same time.
be one of the crowd	/wʌn əv ðə 'kraʊd/	in der Masse untergehen	Arty people don't like to be thought of as **one of the crowd**.

raise a smile	/ˌreɪz ə ˈsmaɪl/	ein Lächeln hervorrufen	Tacky postcards often **raise a smile**.
regardless of	/rɪˈgɑːdləs ˌəv/	ungeachtet	**Regardless of** my preparations the journey was hellish.
run the risk of	/ˌrʌn ðə ˈrɪsk əv/	etwas riskieren	Indecisive people **run the risk of** seeming unadventurous.
take delight in	/ˌteɪk dɪˈlaɪt ɪn/	Freude daran finden	My parents **took delight in** telling me how awful I was as a child.
undivided attention	/ˌʌndɪvaɪdɪd əˈtenʃn/	ungeteilte Aufmerksamkeit	Kids always want your **undivided attention**.
with a view to doing sth	/wɪð ə ˌvjuː tə ˈduːɪŋ sʌmθɪŋ/	mit der Absicht, etwas zu tun	The postcard combines several different pictures **with a view to pleasing everyone**.
You can't go wrong with ...	/jə ˌkaːnt gəʊ ˈrɒŋ wɪð/	Mit ... kann man nichts falsch machen.	**You can't go wrong with** a pint of Guinness.

Unit 9

The perfect face (p. 78–79)

appealing (adj)	/əˈpiːlɪŋ/	anziehend	He has a very **appealing** smile.
arched (adj)	/ɑːtʃt/	geschwungen	A lot of film stars and models have **arched** eyebrows.
baby-faced (adj)	/ˈbeɪbɪˌfeɪst/	mit einem Milchgesicht	A lot of women like **baby-faced** men.
composite (adj)	/ˈkɒmpəzɪt/	zusammengestellt	The computer created two **composite** pictures.
cute (adj) (TS)	/kjuːt/	niedlich	I love dimples – they're so **cute**.
expressive (adj)	/ɪkˈspresɪv/	ausdrucksvoll	She has very **expressive** eyes.
key (adj)	/kiː/	Schlüssee-	Dr Perrett conducted one or two **key** experiments.
objective (adj)	/ɒbˈdʒektɪv/	objektiv	Do you think that beauty is **objective**?
plump (adj)	/plʌmp/	rundlich	Black people seem to prefer **plumper** faces.
prominent (adj)	/ˈprɒmɪnənt/	hervorstehend	Most people find **prominent** cheekbones attractive.
quantifiable (adj)	/ˌkwɒntɪˈfaɪəbl/	messbar	Do you agree that beauty is **quantifiable**?
sparkling (adj)	/ˈspɑːklɪŋ/	glänzend	**Sparkling** eyes are generally considered attractive.
top-ranking (adj)	/ˈtɒpˌrænkɪŋ/	höchstplatziert	The **top-ranking** male face had gentle features.
trustworthy (adj)	/ˈtrʌstwɜːðɪ/	zuverlässig	Women think that men with feminine faces are more **trustworthy**.
turned-up (adj)	/ˌtɜːndˈʌp/	Stups-	Do you like **turned-up** noses?
adage (n)	/ˈædɪdʒ/	Spruch	Do you believe in the old **adage** 'Beauty is in the eye of the beholder'?
bone structure (n)	/ˈbəʊn ˌstrʌktʃə(r)/	Knochenbau	Good **bone structure** makes a face attractive.
cheekbone (n)	/ˈtʃiːkbəʊnz/	Wangenknochen	High **cheekbone**s are attractive.
cultural boundary (n)	/ˌkʌltʃərəl ˈbaʊndrɪ/	Kulturgrenze	Do ideals of beauty cross **cultural boundaries**?
dimples (n pl)	/ˈdɪmplz/	Grübchen	When he smiles he gets **dimples** in his cheeks.
jaw (n)	/dʒɔː/	Kiefer	He has a square **jaw**.
rating (n)	/ˈreɪtɪŋ/	Bewertungsziffer	Volunteers were asked to give each of the photos an attractiveness **rating**.
scar (n)	/skɑː(r)/	Narbe	In some cultures **scars** are considered attractive.
tattoo (n)	/təˈtuː/	Tätowierung	What do you think of people with **tattoos**?

put forward (phr v)	/ˌpʊt ˈfɔːwəd/	vorbringen	Dr Perrett **puts forward** an evolutionary theory to explain this preference.
challenge (v)	/ˈtʃælɪndʒ/	anzweifeln	He **challenge**s accepted theories of beauty.
process (v)	/ˈprəʊses/	bearbeiten	Computers can **process** vast quantities of data.
rank (v)	/ræŋk/	einstufen	Photos of women were **ranked** for their attractiveness.
swoon (v)	/swuːn/	schwärmen	Why do women **swoon** over stars like Tom Cruise and Leonardo DiCaprio?
at first glance	/ət ˌfɜːst ˈglɑːns/	auf den ersten Blick	**At first glance,** the faces looked very similar.
Beauty is in the eye of the beholder.	/ˈbjuːtɪ ɪz ɪn ðɪ ˌaɪ əv ðə bɪˈhəʊldə(r)/	Die Schönheit Liegt im Auge des Betrachters.	Romantics believe that **beauty is in the eye of the beholder.**
by and large	/ˌbaɪ ən ˈlɑːdʒ/	im Großen und Ganzen	**By and large,** we all seem to be attracted to the same things.

Cosmetic surgery (p. 80–81)

ageing (adj) (TS)	/ˈeɪdʒɪŋ/	alternd	**Ageing** film-stars who've had cosmetic surgery all look the same.
commonplace (adj)	/ˈkɒmənpleɪs/	üblich	Cosmetic surgery is becoming more and more **commonplace**.
grateful (adj)	/ˈgreɪtfl/	dankbar	We should be **grateful** for what God has given us.
indulgent (adj)	/ɪnˈdʌldʒənt/	sich Luxus erlauben	Do you think it's **indulgent** to spend money on cosmetic surgery?
inner (adj) (TS)	/ˈɪnə(r)/	innerlich	Do you agree that the most beautiful women are the ones whose **inner** beauty shines out?
pert (adj)	/pɜːt/	keck	Cindy wanted a **pert,** turned-up nose.
cosmetic surgery (n)	/kɒzˌmetɪk ˈsɜːdʒərɪ/	Schönheitsoperation	Do you know anyone who has had **cosmetic surgery**?
eyesight (n)	/ˈaɪsaɪt/	Sehvermögen	Does eating carrots improve your **eyesight**?
looks (n) (TS)	/lʊks/	Aussenhein	Rita thinks that Jean's **looks** helped her to get her job.
nose job (n)	/ˈnəʊz ˌdʒɒb/	Nasenkorrektur	How many **nose job**s did Cindy have?
nostril (n)	/ˈnɒstrəl/	Nasenflügel	They made her **nostril**s smaller.
poverty (n)	/ˈpɒvətɪ/	Armut	Is it right to have cosmetic surgery when there's so much **poverty** in the world?
sunscreen (n)	/ˈsʌnskriːn/	Sonnenblende	You should wear **sunscreen** to protect your skin against the sun.
shine out (phr v)	/ʃaɪn ˈaʊt/	sich deutlich zeigen	I like people whose inner beauty **shines out**.
highlight (v)	/ˈhaɪlaɪt/	Strähnchen machen	Have you ever had your hair **highlighted**?
straighten (v)	/ˈstreɪtn/	gerade stellen	Some people choose to have their teeth **straightened** at the dentist's.
widen (v)	/ˈwaɪdn/	weit machen	First of all, she had her eyes **widened**.
be embodied in	/biː emˈbɒdɪd ɪn/	verkörpert sein in	She wanted the sort of features that **are embodied in** dolls like Barbie and Cindy.
be influenced by (TS)	/biː ˈɪnfluːənst ˌbaɪ/	sich beeinflussen Lassen durch	We shouldn't **be influenced by** stereotypical ideas of beauty.
hang on (TS)	/ˌhæŋ ˈɒn/	warte mal	**Hang on**, Rita. We have to make the distinction between health and beauty.
have one's nose done (TS)	/hæv wʌnz ˈnəʊz ˌdʌn/	seine Nase herrichten lassen	**Having your nose done** only costs the price of a vacation.
It doesn't get you anywhere.	/ɪt ˌdʌznt ˌget juː ˈenɪweə(r)/	Man hat keinen Vorteil davon.	Before, having a genius IQ **didn't get me anywhere**.
It is reckoned (that)	/ɪt ɪz ˈrekənd (ðæt)/	Es wird angenommen, (dass)	**It is reckoned that** our capital city has the highest crime rate in the country.
It is sometimes assumed (that)	/ɪt ɪz ˌsʌmtaɪmz əˈsjuːmd (ðæt)/	Manchmal geht man davon aus, (dass)	**It is sometimes assumed** that all unmarried women are looking for a husband.
That's where I disagree. (TS)	/ˌðæts weə(r) aɪ ˌdɪsəˈgriː/	Damit bin ich nicht einverstanden.	There's nothing wrong with trying to improve on what nature has given you.' **'That's where I disagree.'**

Speed dating (p. 82–84)

bubbly (adj)	/'bʌblɪ/	überschäumend	Kevin thought Sindy was **bubbly** and lively.
dizzy (adj)	/'dɪzɪ/	verworren	Someone who is **dizzy** is not very practical.
down-to-earth (adj)	/ˌdaʊntuː'ɜːθ/	nüchtern, bodenständig	I like practical, **down-to-earth** people.
drippy (adj)	/'drɪpɪ/	fade	Someone who is **drippy** seems weak and not very interesting.
harmless (adj)	/'hɑːmləs/	harmlos	He was **harmless** but not very inspiring.
laddish (adj)	/'lædɪʃ/	machohaft	Men who are **laddish** are mainly interested in hobbies considered to be typically male.
laid-back (adj)	/ˌleɪd'bæk/	gelassen	People who are **laid-back** never seem to worry about things.
level-headed (adj)	/ˌlevəl'hedɪd/	ausgeglichen	I prefer people who are down-to-earth and **level-headed**.
obsessive (adj)	/ɒb'sesɪv/	besessen	**Obsessive** people are difficult to deal with.
open-minded (adj)	/ˌəʊpən'maɪndəd/	unvoreingenommen	I wish my parents were more **open-minded** and tolerant.
outgoing (adj)	/ˌaʊt'gəʊɪŋ/	kontaktfreudig	She's a friendly **outgoing** person.
potential (adj)	/pə'tenʃl/	möglich(e)	You can meet five **potential** mates in less than half an hour.
self-centred (adj)	/ˌself'sentəd/	egozentrisch	She was very **self-centred** and didn't ask me any questions about myself.
spaced out (adj)	/ˌspeɪst 'aʊt/	benommen	Someone who is **spaced out** does not seem quite aware of what is happening around them.
stand-offish (adj)	/ˌstænd'ɒfɪʃ/	zurückhaltend	Jim thought Claire was **stand-offish** and not very friendly.
straight (adj)	/streɪt/	spießig	Someone who is **straight** seems conventional and boring.
unpretentious (adj)	/ˌʌnprɪ'tenʃəs/	anspruchslos	**Unpretentious** people are down-to-earth and not at all snobbish.
blind date (n)	/ˌblaɪnd 'deɪt/	Blind Date (Rendezvous mit jmd, den man nicht kennt)	Have you ever been on a **blind date**?
manners (n pl)	/'mænəz/	Manieren	Craig thought Erica had awful **manners**.
mate (n)	/meɪt/	Partner	Speed dating enables you to meet several potential **mate**s in a short period.
suffering (n)	/'sʌfərɪŋ/	Kummer	If you don't like the person you meet, the **suffering** will be over after five minutes.
break up (with)	/ˌbreɪk 'ʌp (wɪð)/	sich trennen (von)	Adam **broke up** with his girlfriend three months ago.
ramble on (phr v)	/ˌræmbl 'ɒn/	schwafeln	She **rambled on** too much about her home town in Ireland.
sign up (for) (phr v)	/saɪn 'ʌp (fə(r))/	sich anmelden für	Five men and five women had **signed up** for the event.
turn off (phr v)	/ˌtɜːn 'ɒf/	stören, anwidern an	What would **turn** you **off** somebody immediately?
materialise (v)	/mə'tɪərɪə'laɪz/	etwas werden	Nothing **materialised** from his previous relationships.
absorbed with oneself	/əb'zɔːbd wɪð wʌnself/	von sich eingenommen	Craig thought Erica was very **absorbed with herself**.
be after sb	/biː 'ɑːftə/	auf der Suche nach jmd. sein	Adam **is after someone** who is a good laugh.
be out and about	/biː ˌaʊt ən ə'baʊt/	mit jmd. beschäftigt sein	Tony doesn't often meet anyone when **he's out and about**.
a bit of a laugh	/ə ˌbɪt əv ə 'lɑːf/	ein bisschen Spaß	Jim just wants **a bit of a laugh**.
fall for each other	/ˌfɔːl fə(r) iːtʃ 'ʌðə(r)/	sich ineinander verlieben	Which of the couples **fell for each other**?
a good laugh	/ə ˌgʊd 'lɑːf/	jmd. zum Lachen	I want someone who's **a good laugh**.
not on the same planet	/ˌnɒt ɒn ðə ˌseɪm 'plænɪt/	nicht die gleiche Wellenlänge haben	I had nothing in common with her – we just weren't **on the same planet**.

on sight	/ɒn ˈsaɪt/	auf den ersten Blick	If you hate each other **on sight,** the suffering will only last five minutes.
safe in the knowledge (that)	/ˌseɪf ɪn ðə ˈnɒlɪdʒ (ðət)/	sicher, dass	You can be **safe in the knowledge** that the suffering won't go on forever.

Blind Date (p. 85–86)

big-headed (adj) (TS)	/bɪɡˈhedɪd/	eingebildet	She thought James was **big-headed.**
cunning (adj) (TS)	/ˈkʌnɪŋ/	listig	A **cunning** person deceives people in order to get what they want.
foxy (adj) (TS)	/ˈfɒksɪ/	rotbraun	Number 1 describes herself as sly, cunning and naturally **foxy.**
immature (adj) (TS)	/ˌɪməˈtjʊə(r)/	unreif	He's not my type – he's too **immature.**
self-obsessed (adj) (TS)	/ˌselfɒbˈsest/	mit sich selbst beschäftigt	Mel thought James was big-headed and **self-obsessed.**
shipwrecked (adj)	/ˈʃɪprekt/	Schiffbruch erlitten haben	If you were **shipwrecked** on a desert island, what three possessions would you want to have with you?
sly (adj) (TS)	/slaɪ/	hinterhältig	You can't trust her – she's **sly.**
body language (n) (TS)	/ˈbɒdɪ ˌlæŋɡwɪdʒ/	Körpersprache	**Body language** reveals a lot about your emotions.
caterpillar (n)	/ˈkætəpɪlə(r)/	Raupe	His eyebrows reminded her of **caterpillars.**
contestant (n)	/kənˈtestənt/	Teilnehmer	Each player asks three questions to three hidden **contestant**s.
gypsy (n) (TS)	/ˈdʒɪpsɪ/	Zigeuner(in)	She had her palm read by a **gypsy.**
man-eater (n) (TS)	/ˈmæniːtə(r)/	männermordende Frau	A **man-eater** is a woman who has relationships with a lot of different men.
man-eating tiger (n) (TS)	/ˌmæniːtɪŋ ˈtaɪɡə(r)/	menschenfressender Tiger	Number 3 describes herself as a **man-eating tiger.**
get on (phr v)	/ˌɡet ˈɒn/	(miteinander) zurechtkommen	Couples come back to the show a week later to tell the audience how they **got on.**
go after (phr v) (TS)	/ɡəʊ ˈɑːftə(r)/	nachstreben	When I **go after** something there's no escape.
go back (phr v) (TS)	/ɡəʊ ˈbæk/	zurücksetzen	What did you think of James when the screen **went back**?
give away (phr v) (TS)	/ɡɪv əˈweɪ/	verraten	Body language tends to **give** people **away.**
keep up with (phr v) (TS)	/kiːp ˈʌp wɪð/	Schritt halten mit	You'll need all your strength to **keep up with** me!
fancy (v)	/ˈfænsɪ/	gefallen, mögen	Do Mel and James **fancy** each other?
host (v)	/həʊst/	präsentieren	The show is **hosted** by Cilla Black.
reflect (v)	/rɪˈflekt/	widerspiegeln	Do you think people's pets **reflect** their personality?
run (v)	/rʌn/	laufen	The show has been **running** since 1985.
assuming (that)	/əˈsjuːmɪŋ (ðət)/	vorausgesetzt, dass	**Assuming** that you had plenty of money, what countries would you like to visit?
be all over sb like a rash (TS)	/biː ɔːl ˌəʊvə sʌmbədɪ laɪk ə ˈræʃ/	jmd. übertrieben leidenschaftlich begrüßen	Mel was **all over me like a rash.**
come alive	/kʌm əˈlaɪv/	aufblühen	I tend to **come alive** in the evenings.
come true	/kʌm ˈtruː/	Wirklichkeit werden	Do you believe that dreams can **come true**?
go well (TS)	/ɡəʊ ˈwel/	gut gehen	Did Mel and James think their date **went well**?
have one's palm read (TS)	/hæv wʌnz ˈpɑːm ˌred/	sich die Hand Lesen Lassen	Have you ever **had your palm read** by a gypsy?
Money is no object.	/ˌmʌnɪ ɪz nəʊ ˈɒbdʒekt/	Geld spielt keine Rolle.	They could go wherever they wanted on holiday – **money is no object.**
not be sb's type (TS)	/nɒt biː sʌmbədɪz ˈtaɪp/	nicht jemands Typ sein	James **wasn't my type** – he was too immature.

on the basis of	/ɒn ðə ˈbeɪsɪs əv/	auf der Grundlage von	The player must choose a contestant **on the basis of** his/her answers.
supposing (that)	/səˈpəʊzɪŋ ðət/	angenommen, dass	**Supposing that** you could go out with anyone in the world, who would it be?
the way to a man's heart	/ðə ˌweɪ tuː ə mænz ˌhɑːt/	Liebe geht durch den Magen	Is one of **the ways to James' heart** through his stomach?

Never Ever (p. 87)

low (adj) (TS)	/ləʊ/	unglücklich	She's feeling sad and **low**.
sane (adj)	/seɪn/	(geistig) gesund	Your answers will keep me **sane**.
soul (n)	/səʊl/	Seele	I've searched my **soul** for the answer.
either way	/ˌaɪðə ˈweɪ/	wie dem auch sei	**Either way,** I must know the answer.
feel at ease	/fiːl ət ˈiːz/	sich wohl fühlen	It's important to **feel at ease**.
go out of one's mind	/gəʊ ˌaʊt əv wʌnz ˈmaɪnd/	seinen Verstand verlieren	She's **going out of her mind** with sadness.
in a daze	/ɪn ə ˈdeɪz/	betäubt	She feels confused and **in a daze**.
in a black hole	/ɪn ə ˌblæk ˈhəʊl/	in einem schwarzen Loch	I feel depressed – as if I'm **in a black hole**.
peace of mind	/piːs əv ˈmaɪnd/	Gemütsruhe	I need to know the answers for my **peace of mind**.
start a fight	/ˌstɑːt ə ˈfaɪt/	einen Streit anfangen	I don't want to quarrel or **start a fight**.
tell sb sth to their face	/tel sʌmbədɪ sʌmθɪŋ tə ðeə ˈfeɪs/	jmd. etwas ins Gesicht sagen	You should **tell her what she did wrong to her face**.
treat you right	/ˌtriːt juː ˈraɪt/	jmd. gut behandeln	I always tried to **treat you right**.

33

Unit 10

The genius of the Guggenheim (p. 88–89)

eager (adj)	/ˈiːgə(r)/	versessen auf	He was **eager** to establish a European base for the Guggenheim.
eccentric (adj)	/ɪkˈsentrɪk/	exzentrisch	Gehry fell in love with the **eccentric** Basque city.
growing (adj)	/ˈgrəʊɪŋ/	zunehmend	They wanted an art museum to cement the city's **growing** reputation.
hideous (adj)	/ˈhɪdɪəs/	scheußlich	Bilbao is surrounded by a **hideous** urban sprawl.
newly appointed (adj)	/ˌnjuːlɪ əˈpɔɪntəd/	neu ernannt	Thomas Krens was the **newly appointed** director of the Guggenheim foundation.
post-industrial (adj)	/ˌpəʊstɪnˈdʌstrɪəl/	postindustriell	Gehry revelled in the **post-industrial** environment.
riverside (adj)	/ˈrɪvəsaɪd/	an einem Fluss	Bilbao is a **riverside** city.
run-down (adj)	/ˌrʌnˈdaʊn/	heruntergekommen	There are a lot of **run-down** buildings in the city.
semi-derelict (adj)	/ˌsemɪˈderəlɪkt/	halb verlassen	While out running he noticed a **semi-derelict** waterfront zone.
shipbuilding (adj)	/ˈʃɪpbɪldɪŋ/	Schiffsbau-	Bilbao is a former **shipbuilding** community.
space-age (adj)	/ˈspeɪseɪdʒ/	futuristisch	It's a post-modern, **space-age** museum.
sprawling (adj)	/ˈsprɔːlɪŋ/	sich in alle Richtungen ausbreitend	Bilbao is a large **sprawling** city.
tough (adj)	/tʌf/	hart	It used to be a **tough** shipbuilding community.

waterfront (adj)	/'wɔːtəfrʌnt/	Ufer-	The museum is built on a **waterfront** zone.
wine-bottling (adj)	/'waɪnbɒtlɪŋ/	Wein abfüllend	The site proposed originally was a former **wine-bottling** warehouse.
brainchild (n)	/'breɪntʃaɪld/	geistiges Erbe	The Guggenheim is the **brainchild** of Thomas Krens.
non-starter (n)	/nɒn'stɑːtə(r)/	etwas Aussichtsloses	The site proposed originally was a **non-starter**.
redevelopment programme (n)	/riːdɪ'veləpmənt ˌprəʊgræm/	Erneuerungsprogramm	In the 1980s the Basque government began a **redevelopment programme** for Bilbao.
terminal (n)	/'tɜːmɪnl/	Ankunfts-, Wartehalle	There were plans to build a new airport **terminal**.
urban sprawl (n)	/ˌɜːbən 'sprɔːl/	wild wuchernde Ausbreitung des Stadtgebietes	The Guggenheim looks like a shiny toy surrounded by hideous **urban sprawl**.
face out (phr v)	/feɪs 'aʊt/	Blick haben auf	Bilbao **faces out** onto the Bay of Biscay.
revel in (phr v)	/ˌrevəl 'ɪn/	etwas sehr genießen	Gehry **revelled in** the dirt and chaos of the environment.
wind through (phr v)	/'waɪnd ˌθruː/	sich schlängeln durch	You leave the airport and **wind through** the green hills.
cement (v)	/sɪ'ment/	verstärken	The Basque regional government wanted to **cement** the city's growing reputation.
commission (v)	/kə'mɪʃn/	beauftragen	They **commissioned** the best possible people for the job.
glimpse (v)	/glɪmps/	einen Blick erhaschen	The Guggenheim can be **glimpsed** in the distance from the hills.
overlook (v)	/ˌəʊvə'lʊk/	auf etwas sehen	The Jesuit University **overlooks** the river Nervion.
possess (v)	/pə'zes/	dazu bringen	What **possessed** the museum to come to a place like Bilbao?
realise (v)	/'rɪəlaɪz/	verwirklichen	Californian architect Frank Gehry was the man chosen to **realise** the project.
at every turn	/ət ˌevrɪ 'tɜːn/	in jeder Hinsicht	The museum dominates the city **at every turn**.
the best and brightest	/ðə ˌbest ən 'braɪtəst/	die Besten und die Gescheitesten	They commissioned **the best and brightest** in the international architectural world.
by chance	/baɪ 'tʃɑːns/	zufällig	**By chance,** Krens found the ideal site.
It's well worth ...	/ɪts ˌwel 'wɜːθ/	Es ist ... wert.	The Bilbao Guggenheim **is well worth** a visit.
like no other	/ˌlaɪk nəʊ 'ʌðə(r)/	einzigartig	It's a contemporary art museum **like no other**.
What on earth ...?	/ˌwɒt ɒn 'ɜːθ/	Was in Gottes Namen ...?	**What on earth** possessed the Guggenheim Museum to come to Bilbao?
with this in mind	/wɪð ˌðɪs ɪn 'maɪnd/	mit diesem Gedanken	Krens wanted to establish a European base for the Guggenheim, and **with this in mind,** he came to Bilbao.

Frida Kahlo (p. 91–92)

cropped (adj) (TS)	/krɒpt/	kurzgeschnitten	The second painting shows Frida with **cropped** hair.
devastated (adj)	/'devəsˌteɪtəd/	erschüttert	Frida was **devastated** during her separation from Diego.
extramarital (adj)	/ˌekstrə'mærɪtl/	außerehelich	They both had **extramarital** affairs.
unfaithful (adj)	/ʌn'feɪθfl/	untreu	Diego was often **unfaithful** to her.
highly (adv) (TS)	/'haɪlɪ/	hoch-	Diego was both **highly** intelligent and very rich.
ironically (adv)	/aɪ'rɒnɪklɪ/	ironischerweise	**Ironically,** she painted some of her most powerful works during their separation.
affair (n)	/ə'feə(r)/	Affäre	Diego even had an **affair** with her younger sister.
divorce proceedings (n pl)	/dɪ'vɔːs prəˌsiːdɪŋz/	Ehescheidungsverfahren	On Frida's return to Mexico, the couple began **divorce proceedings**.
dove (n)	/dʌv/	Taube	The **dove** is a white bird, often thought of as the symbol of peace.
handrail (n)	/'hændreɪl/	Geländer	Her body was pierced by a **handrail** in a streetcar accident.

interpretation (n)	/ɪntɜːprɪ'teɪʃn/	Interpretation	What's your **interpretation** of the paintings?
landscape (n)	/'lændskeɪp/	Landschaftsgemälde	A **landscape** is a painting of an area of land, usually in the countryside.
laser treatment (n)	/'leɪzə ˌtriːtmənt/	Laserbehandlung	**Laser treatment** is often used for treating health problems.
medical expenses (n pl)	/'medɪkl ɪkˌspensəz/	die Kosten für medizinische Hilfe	In the end, Frida's father was unable to pay her **medical expenses**.
spine (n)	/spaɪn/	Wirbelsäule	In 1946 Frida had surgery on her **spine**.
still life (n)	/ˌstɪl 'laɪf/	Still Leben	A **still life** is a painting of an arrangement of objects, often flowers or fruit.
streetcar (n) (Am E)	/'striːtkɑː(r)/	Straßenbahn	She was badly injured in a **streetcar** accident.
surgery (n)	/həv sɜːdzərɪ/	Operation	Have you ever had **surgery**?
wheelchair (n)	/'wiːltʃeə(r)/	Rollstuhl	Christopher Reeve has been confined to a **wheelchair** since the accident.
cut off (phr v) (TS)	/ˌkʌt 'ɒf/	abschneiden	Did she **cut off** her hair to symbolise equality?
hand in (phr v)	/ˌhænd 'ɪn/	abgeben	The keys were **handed in** at Lost Property.
make out (phr v) (TS)	/ˌmeɪk 'aʊt/	begreifen	It's hard to **make out** what some of the paintings are about.
run away (from) (phr v)	/ˌrʌn ə'weɪ (frəm)/	wegrennen (von)	Do you think the man in Picture c) is **running away** from someone?
work out (phr v) (TS)	/ˌwɜːk 'aʊt/	funktionieren	Their marriage didn't **work out** too well.
amputate (v)	/'æmpjəteɪt/	amputieren	In 1953 her right leg was **amputated** below the knee.
claim (v)	/kleɪm/	behaupten	Frida **claimed** her birthdate as 1910, the year of the Mexican Revolution.
conceal (v)	/kən'siːl/	verbergen	She always **concealed** her right leg.
contract (v)	/kən'trækt/	sich etwas zuziehen	She **contracted** polio when she was six years old.
day-dream (v)	/'deɪdrːm/	tagträumen	Sorry, I didn't hear you. I must have been **day-dreaming**.
deteriorate (v) (TS)	/dɪ'tɪərɪəreɪt/	sich verschlechtern	She painted Roots when her health was beginning to **deteriorate**.
exile (v)	/'eksaɪl· egzaɪ/	verbannen	She had an affair with Trotsky when he was **exiled** from the Soviet Union.
pierce (v)	/pɪəs/	durchbohren	Her body was **pierced** by a handrail in a streetcar accident.
reckon (v) (TS)	/'rekən/	vermuten	I **reckon** Diego must have been very rich or very intelligent.
remarry (v)	/ˌriː'mærɪ/	sich wiederverheiraten	Diego and Frida **remarried** in December 1940.
tease (v)	/tiːz/	hänseln	The other children **teased** her about her leg.
undergo (v)	/ˌʌndə'gəʊ/	sich unterziehen	She **underwent** thirty-two major operations.
at first (TS)	/ət 'fɜːst/	zuerst	**At first**, Frida's father was against the marriage.
be confined to	/bɪ kən'faɪnd tə/	eingeschränkt sein auf	She **was confined to** her room for nine months.
Cheer up!	/ˌtʃɪə(r) 'ʌp/	Kopf hoch!	**Cheer up!** Things aren't that bad, are they?
have sth to do with sth (TS)	/hæv ˌsʌmθɪŋ tə ˌduː wɪð ˌsʌmθɪŋ/	etwas damit zu tun haben	Does the painting **have something to do with women's liberation**?
not be much of a (TS)	/nɒt bɪ 'mʌtʃ əv ə/	nicht viel bedeuten als	He **can't be much of a** painter.
ups and downs	/ˌʌps ən 'daʊnz/	Höhen und Tiefen	Their marriage certainly had its **ups and downs**.

Eureka/Dream invention (p. 93–94)

dreadful (adj) (TS)	/'dredfl/	schrecklich	AIDS is a **dreadful** disease.
humiliating (adj) (TS)	/hjuː'mɪlɪeɪtɪŋ/	erniedrigend	Baylis found it **humiliating** going round all the companies.

English	Pronunciation	German	Example
non-fattening (adj)	/ˌnɒnˈfætnɪŋ/	nicht dick machend	It would be great if chocolate and ice cream were **non-fattening**.
personalised (adj)	/ˈpɜːsənəlaɪzd/	persönlich	There was a **personalised** message attached to the flowers.
raunchy (adj) (TS)	/ˈrɔːntʃɪ/	aufreizend, erotisch	I dreamed I was listening to some **raunchy** song by Dame Nellie Melba.
rusty (adj) (TS)	/ˈrʌstɪ/	rostig	The needle on the gramophone player looks like a **rusty** nail.
wind-up (adj) (TS)	/ˈwaɪndʌp/	aufziehbar	Have you ever seen an old **wind-up** gramophone?
horrendously (adv) (TS)	/həˈrendəslɪ/	grauenhaft	Electricity in the form of batteries is **horrendously** expensive.
backer (n)	/ˈbækə(r)/	Geldgeber	It was hard finding a **backer** at first.
backside (n) (TS)	/ˈbæksaɪd/	Hintern	He decided to get off his **backside** and do something.
confidentiality agreement (n) (TS)	/ˌkɒnfɪˌdenʃɪˈælətɪ əgriːmənt/	Geheimhaltungsversprechen	He approached lots of British companies with a **confidentiality agreement**.
contact lens (n)	/ˈkɒntækt ˌlenz/	Kontaktlinse	Do you wear **contact lens**es?
device (n)	/dɪˈvaɪs/	Apparat	Would you like a car with an automatic self-parking **device**?
the disabled (n pl) (TS)	/ðə dɪsˈeɪbld/	Behinderte	He invented a range of products for **the disabled**.
domestic appliances (n pl) (TS)	/dəˌmestɪk əˈplaɪənsɪz/	Haushaltsgeräte	Baylis kept old **domestic appliances** in his shed.
funding (n)	/ˈfʌndɪŋ/	finanzielle Unterstützung	It was important to get **funding** for the project.
graveyard (n) (TS)	/ˈgreɪvjɑːd/	Friedhof	His shed was a **graveyard** of domestic appliances.
monocle (n) (TS)	/ˈmɒnəkl/	Monokel	A **monocle** is a lens that you wear on one eye.
the needy (n pl)	/ðə ˈniːdɪ/	Mittellose	He gets satisfaction from the fact that Baygen products help **the needy**.
number (n) (TS)	/ˈnʌmbə(r)/	Nummer	He dreamed he was listening to a raunchy **number** by Dame Nellie Melba.
passion (n)	/ˈpæʃn/	Leidenschaft	Inventing things is Trevor Baylis' **passion**.
the physically handicapped (n pl)	/ˌfɪzɪklɪ ˈhændɪkæpt/	Körperbehinderte	He enjoys inventing products that might help **the physically handicapped**.
pith helmet (n) (TS)	/ˈpɪθ ˌhelmɪt/	Tropenhelm	A **pith helmet** protects your head from the sun.
prototype (n)	/ˈprəʊtətaɪp/	Prototyp	How long did it take to get the **prototype**?
range (n) (TS)	/reɪndʒ/	Reihe	A **range** of products for the disabled had previously been stolen from him.
shed (n) (TS)	/ʃed/	Scheune	His **shed** contained lots of domestic appliances.
spread (n)	/spred/	Verbreitung	The only way to stop the **spread** of AIDS is to educate people about the disease.
spring (n) (TS)	/sprɪŋ/	Feder	There's enough power in a **spring** to drive a small dynamo.
zip (n)	/zɪp/	Reißverschluss	When was the first **zip** invented?
doze off (phr v)	/dəʊz ˈɒf/	einschlafen	Baylis **dozed off** and had a dream.
share in (phr v) (TS)	/ˈʃeə(r) ɪn/	Anteil haben an	The company from South Africa was willing to help, provided that they could **share in** his success.
talk down to (phr v) (TS)	/tɔːk ˈdaʊn tə/	herablassend sprechen mit jmd.	The people he approached all **talked down to** him.
drag (v) (TS)	/dræg/	schleifen, ziehen	Amazing to think you can play music by **dragging** a rusty nail round a piece of bakelite.
drive (v) (TS)	/draɪv/	antreiben	A small dynamo would **drive** the radio.
file (v)	/faɪl/	einreichen	He decide to **file** for a patent.
outstrip (v)	/ˌaʊtˈstrɪp/	übertreffen	Demand for the radios now **outstrip**s supply.
be stirred to do sth (TS)	/bɪ ˌstɜːd tə ˈduː/	angeregt werden, etwas zu tun	He **was stirred** by his dream **to do something**.
cut its way through (TS)	/ˌkʌt ɪts ˈweɪ ˌθruː/	sich einen Weg bahnen	The AIDS epidemic is **cutting its way through** Africa.

First things first. (TS)	/ˌfɜːst ˈθɪŋz ˈfɜːst/	Das Wichtigste zuerst.	**First things first,** before finding a backer I had to file for a patent.
from that point on (TS)	/frəm ˌðæt pɔɪnt ˈɒn/	ab diesem Augenblick	How easy were things **from that point on**?
get (sth) off the ground	/get (sʌmθɪŋ) ˌɒf ðə ˈgraʊnd/	etwas von Grund auf aufbauen	It took him two to three months to **get a prototype off the ground.**

Word families/Close up (p. 95–96)

be crammed with (adj)	/bɪ ˈkræmd wɪð/	mit etwas vollgestopft sein	The paper **was crammed with** figures.
failed (adj)	/feɪld/	gescheitert	Fry obtained some of the **failed** glue and made bookmarks with it.
frantic (adj)	/ˈfræntɪk/	verzweifelt	He used to have a **frantic** search for the right page.
high-frequency (adj)	/ˌhaɪˈfriːkwənsɪ/	Hochfrequenz-	The peanut bar had been affected by **high-frequency** emissions.
intrigued (adj)	/ɪnˈtriːgd/	fasziniert	Dr Spencer was **intrigued** to find out more.
melted (adj)	/ˈmeltəd/	geschmolzen	The sticky substance in his pocket turned out to be a **melted** peanut bar.
prospective (adj)	/prəˈspektɪv/	zukünftig	Salesmen demonstrate their products to **prospective** customers.
sticky (adj)	/ˈstɪkɪ/	klebrig	He felt something **sticky** in his pocket.
drastically (adv)	/ˈdræstɪklɪ/	drastisch	The price of electronic equipment has been **drastically** reduced over the past few years.
inevitably (adv)	/ɪnˈevɪtəblɪ/	zwangsläufig	**Inevitably,** he could never find the right page when he needed to.
advances (n pl)	/ədˈvɑːnsɪz/	Fortschritt	There have been huge technological **advances** in recent years.
bookmark (n)	/ˈbʊkmɑːk/	Lesezeichen	Some people use Post-its as **bookmark**s.
chemical weapons (n pl)	/ˌkemɪkl ˈwepənz/	chemische Waffen	Do you agree with the use of **chemical weapons**?
choir (n)	/ˈkwaɪə(r)/	Chor	Fry was a member of a church **choir**.
emissions (n pl)	/ɪˈmɪʃnz/	Strahlung	High-frequency radio **emissions** can be very harmful.
equation (n)	/ɪˈkweɪʒn/	Gleichung	I never really understood mathematical **equation**s.
genetic engineering (n)	/dʒənetɪk ˌendʒɪˈnɪərɪŋ/	Gentechnik	Do you agree with the idea of **genetic engineering**?
glue (n)	/gluː/	Klebstoff	One of Fry's research colleagues had made a **glue**.
hymnbook (n)	/ˈhɪmbʊk/	Gesangsbuch	Fry could never find the right place in his **hymnbook**.
ice lolly (n)	/ˌaɪs ˈlɒlɪ/	Eis am Stiel	When he removed the spoon, he found he had an **ice lolly**.
impact (n)	/ˈɪmpækt/	Einfluss	What sort of an **impact** did unemployment have on your life?
mass destruction (n)	/ˌmæs dɪˈstrʌkʃn/	Massenvernichtung	Nuclear weapons are weapons of **mass destruction**.
microwave (oven) (n)	/ˈmaɪkrəweɪv/	Mikrowelle	Do you have a **microwave** at home?
peanut bar (n)	/ˈpiːnʌt ˌbɑː(r)/	Erdnussriegel	**Peanut bar**s are usually eaten as snacks.
Post-it note (n)	/ˈpəʊstɪt ˌnəʊt/	Klebezettel	**Post-it note**s are available in several different colours.
salesman (n)	/ˈseɪlzmən/	Vertreter	**Salesmen** often travel long distances.
seaweed (n)	/ˈsiːwiːd/	Seegras	**Seaweed** is a green plant found on beaches.
sermon (n)	/ˈsɜːmən/	Predigt	As he was listening to the **sermon** his mind began to wander.
service (n)	/ˈsɜːvɪs/	Gottesdienst	We sing hymns during the church **service**.
sticking power (n)	/ˈstɪkɪŋ ˌpaʊə(r)/	Klebkraft	The glue had poor **sticking power**.
windowsill (n)	/ˈwɪndəʊsɪl/	Fensterbank	He left the glass of lemonade on the **windowsill**.

drop out (phr v)	/ˌdrɒp ˈaʊt/	herausfallen	The bits of paper always used to **drop out**.
discard (v)	/dɪsˈkɑːd/	verwerfen	The glue had originally been **discarded**.
dismiss (v)	/dɪzˈmɪs/	verwerfen	Until now he had **dismissed** these stories.
install (v)	/ɪnˈstɔːl/	installieren	The first microwave was **installed** in a Boston restaurant.
place (v)	/pleɪs/	stellen	The popcorn was **placed** close to the magnetron.
plunge (v)	/plʌndʒ/	fallen	The temperature **plunged** to below zero.
project (v)	/prəˈdʒekt/	schätzen	Growth in sales is **projected** at nearly 10%.
wander (v)	/ˈwɒndə(r)/	umherschweifen	During the service Fry's mind began to **wander**.
all manner of	/ɔːl ˈmænə(r) əv/	alle Arten von	They can cure **all manner of** conditions.
prove to	/ˈpruːv tə/	sich erweisen als	The glue was discarded when it **proved to** have poor sticking power.
radar-based	/ˈreɪdɑːˌbeɪst/	von Radar unterstützt	He worked on a **radar-based** research project.

Unit 11

The playground pound (p. 98–99)

38

liberating (adj)	/ˈlɪbəreɪtɪŋ/	befreiend	Do you agree that choice is **liberating** for children?
brand (n)	/brænd/	Marke	What **brand** of trainers do you wear?
brand loyalty (n)	/ˌbrænd ˈlɔɪəltɪ/	Markentreue	Advertisers like to encourage **brand loyalty** from an early age.
choice (n)	/tʃɔɪs/	Auswahl	Sally thinks that all the **choice** is bad for children.
consumer (n)	/kənˈsjuːmə(r)/	Verbraucher	Children are being forced to be **consumer**s.
craze (n)	/kreɪz/	Manie	What **craze**s are currently popular in your country?
credibility (n) (TS)	/ˌkredəˈbɪlətɪ/	Glaubwürdigkeit	The concept of playground **credibility** is very important.
jingle (n)	/ˈdʒɪŋgl/	Erkennungsmelodie	Children remember advertising **jingle**s easily.
label (n) (TS)	/ˈleɪbl/	Marke	Is it important to you to wear **label**s?
logo (n)	/ˈləʊgəʊ/	Logo	A **logo** is a small design or symbol used by a company on its products.
marketing potential (n) (TS)	/ˈmɑːkɪtɪŋ pəˌtenʃl/	Marketingmöglichkeit	'Pester power' is an advertiser's term for **marketing potential**.
partnership (n) (TS)	/ˈpɑːtnəʃɪp/	Partnerschaft	Do you think school-business **partnership**s are a good thing?
peer group (n)	/ˈpɪə ˌgruːp/	Gruppe von Gleichaltrigen	Children need to fit in with a **peer group**.
pre-teens (n pl)	/priːˈtiːnz/	junge Teenager	**Pre-teens** are children between 10 and 12.
add up (phr v) (TS)	/ˌæd ˈʌp/	addieren	Children end up having to **add up** burgers in their maths lessons.
fit in (phr v)	/ˌfɪt ˈɪn/	sich anpassen	Do you agree that the right brand helps children **fit in** with a peer group?
look into (phr v) (TS)	/ˌlʊk ˈɪntə/	untersuchen	We're **looking into** promoting products directly in the classroom.
pick up on (phr v) (TS)	/ˌpɪk ˈʌp ɒn/	aufgreifen	Children **pick up on** advertising really fast.
appeal (v) (TS)	/əˈpiːl/	gut ankommen bei	We try to produce adverts that **appeal** to both adults and children.
brainwash (v)	/ˈbreɪnwɒʃ/	einer Gehirnwäsche unterziehen	It's wrong to **brainwash** children.

donate (v)	/dəʊ'neɪt/	spenden	Companies **donate** free equipment to schools in exchange for advertising their products.
exclude (v) (TS)	/ɪk'skluːd/	ausschließen	Kids who wear the wrong brands get **excluded**.
nag (v)	/næg/	quälen	Stop **nagging** me!
pester (v)	/'pestə(r)/	drängen	Have you **pestered** your parents to buy you anything?
promote (v) (TS)	/prə'məʊt/	Werbung machen für	Should companies be allowed to **promote** their products in schools?
subsidise (v) (TS)	/'sʌbsɪdaɪz/	subventionieren	In America schools are actually being **subsidised** by companies.
be required to (TS)	/bɪ rɪ'kwaɪəd tə/	erforderlich sein	Will children one day **be required to** wear Nike trainers before going to school?
from head to toe (TS)	/frəm ˌhed tə 'təʊ/	von Kopf bis Fuß	The children are dressed **from head to toe** in labels.
get it wrong (TS)	/ˌget ɪt 'rɒŋ/	es verkehrt machen	When it comes to brands, children suffer if they **get it wrong**.
a great deal of (TS)	/ə ɡreɪt 'diːl əv/	eine ganze Menge	There's **a great deal of** pressure on parents to buy their children labels.
I tell you what (TS)	/aɪ ˌtel jə 'wɒt/	Weißt du ...	**I tell you what** – if children remembered schoolwork as well as they do advertising, it would be great.
make fun of sb (TS)	/meɪk 'fʌn əv/	jmd. zum Narren halten	Everyone **makes fun of you** if you're not wearing the right trainers.
mind you (TS)	/ˌmaɪnd 'juː/	vergiss nicht	**Mind you**, the situation is worse in America.
the odd one out (TS)	/ðɪ ˌɒd wʌn 'aʊt/	Außenseiter	It's not nice being **the odd one out**.
put a stop to	/ˌpʊt ə 'stɒp tə/	etwas beenden	The government should really **put a stop to** all this.
a sense of identity	/ə ˌsens əv aɪ'dentəti/	Identitätsbewusstsein	Do brands give children **a sense of identity**?
The trick is ... (TS)	/ðə 'trɪk ɪz/	Der Trick ist ...	**The trick is** to make adverts which appeal to both children and adults.

Lexis/Commercials (p. 99–100)

dejected (adj) (TS)	/dɪ'dʒektəd/	entmutigt	The character in the advert gets **dejected** when he gets it all wrong.
advertising agency (n)	/'ædvətaɪzɪŋ 'eɪdʒənsi/	Werbeagentur	Nokes works for an **advertising agency**.
advertising campaign (n)	/'ædvətaɪzɪŋ kæm'peɪn/	Anzeigenkampagne	They ran an effective **advertising campaign**.
advertising executive (n)	/'ædvətaɪzɪŋ ɪg'zekjətɪv/	Leiter der Werbeabteilung	An **advertising executive** specialises in arranging adverts for companies.
availability (n)	/əˌveɪlə'bɪləti/	Verfügbarkeit	What factors influence the **availability** of goods?
brand awareness (n)	/ˌbrænd ə'weənəs/	Markenbewusstsein	**Brand awareness** is increasing among children.
coil (n) (TS)	/kɔɪl/	Trosse	The man had a **coil** of rope over his shoulder.
commercial (n)	/kə'mɜːʃl/	Werbesendung	Do you enjoy watching TV **commercials**?
consumer goods (n pl)	/kən'sjuːmə ˌɡʊdz/	Verbrauchsgüter	Sales of **consumer goods** fell in January.
consumer spending (n)	/kənˌsjuːmə 'spendɪŋ/	Verbraucherausgaben	How do you explain the increase in **consumer spending**?
instant (n) (TS)	/'ɪnstənt/	lösliches Pulver	He doesn't have any coffee apart from a jar of **instant**.
market forces (n pl)	/ˌmɑːkɪt 'fɔːsɪz/	Marktkräfte	**Market forces** determine supply and demand.
market share	/ˌmɑːkɪt 'ʃeə(r)/	Marktanteil	The company is worried that their **market share** might be decreasing.
sales figures (n pl)	/'seɪlz ˌfɪɡəz/	Verkaufszahlen	**Sales figures** are down on last year.
sales force (n)	/'seɪlz ˌfɔːs/	Verkäufer-, Vertreterteam	A **sales force** is a team of people who sell a product.
sales pitch (n)	/'seɪlz ˌpɪtʃ/	Verkaufstechnik	Her **sales pitch** wasn't really appropriate.

slob (n) (TS)	/slɒb/	Waschlappen	Her boyfriend's a lazy **slob**!
blow out (phr v) (TS)	/ˌbləʊ ˈaʊt/	ausblasen	He **blows out** smoke and looks really relaxed.
hand over (phr v) (TS)	/ˌhænd ˈəʊvə(r)/	aushändigen	He **hands over** the chocolates to the gorgeous woman.
fire (v) (TS)	/ˈfaɪə(r)/	abfeuern	He keeps **firing** arrows at people.
miss (v) (TS)	/mɪs/	verfehlen	He fires arrows at people but **misses**.
smash (v) (TS)	/smæʃ/	durchbrechen	His feet **smash** through the window.
get down on one's knees (TS)	/get ˌdaʊn ɒn wʌnz ˈniːz/	sich hinknien	He **gets down on his knees** in front of her.
Never mind. (TS)	/nevə ˈmaɪnd/	Das macht nichts!	Get it? Oh, **never mind**.
a right mess (TS)	/ə ˌraɪt ˈmes/	großer 'Schweinestall'	His flat is **a right mess**.
take one look (TS)	/ˌteɪk wʌn ˈlʊk/	einen Blick werfen auf	He'd **take one look** at the situation and light up.

Commercial breakdown (p. 100–103)

fussy (adj)	/ˈfʌsɪ/	wählerisch	The woman in the advert is **fussy** – she wants a pair of 501s.
haunting (adj)	/ˈhɔːntɪŋ/	ein Ohrwurm	*I heard it through the Grapevine* is a **haunting** song.
male-dominated (adj)	/ˌmeɪlˈdɒmɪneɪtəd/	von Männern dominiert	Is advertising still a **male-dominated** industry?
rugged (adj)	/ˈrʌgɪd/	rau	The young man is a **rugged** individual.
youthful (adj)	/ˈjuːθfl/	jugendlich	It represents **youthful** rebellion.
fiercely (adv)	/ˈfɪəslɪ/	äußerst	It was unusual for a woman to succeed in the **fiercely** male-dominated world of advertising.
ad (n)	/æd/	Anzeige	What do you think of the **ad**?
heart-throb (n)	/ˈhɑːtθrɒb/	Herzensbrecher	Actor Nick Kamen went on to become a **heart-throb**.
launderette (n)	/lɔːnˈdret/	Wäscherei	A **launderette** is a place where you pay to wash your clothes.
positioning (n)	/pəˈzɪʃənɪŋ/	Platzierung	The ad was perfect for Levis' intended **positioning** of their product.
radical chic (n)	/ˌrædɪkl ˈʃiːk/	totale Eleganz	It represents **radical chic**.
rebellion (n)	/rɪˈbeljən/	Aufstand	The advert is all about youthful **rebellion**.
statement (n)	/ˈsteɪtmənt/	Statement	The advert is making a clear **statement**.
storyline (n)	/ˈstɔːrɪlaɪn/	der rote Faden einer Geschichte	It has a very simple **storyline**.
conjure up (phr v)	/ˌkʌndʒə(r) ˈʌp/	heraufbeschwören	The commercial **conjures up** a typical American scene.
hang out (phr v)	/ˌhæŋ ˈaʊt/	heraushängen	His jeans are **hanging out** of the washing machine.
stand for (phr v)	/ˈstænd fə(r)/	etwas repräsentieren	What does the advert **stand for**?
strip off (phr v)	/ˌstrɪp ˈɒf/	sich ausziehen	The young man **strips off** and puts his jeans in the machine.
devote (v)	/dɪˈvəʊt/	widmen	Kamen has several websites **devoted** to him.
epitomise (v)	/ɪˈpɪtəmaɪz/	verkörpern	It **epitomises** everything that is cool.
hit (v)	/hɪt/	treffen	As soon as it **hit** the screens it was a massive success.
release (v)	/rɪˈliːs/	herausbringen	The song was **released** in 1968.
couldn't care less (about)	/ˌkʊdnt keə ˈles (əˌbaʊt)/	etwas ist jmd. egal	He epitomises the rebel who **couldn't care less about** convention.

| new ground | /ˌnjuː ˈɡraʊnd/ | neues Gebiet | The advert established **new ground**. |
| on screen | /ɒn ˈskriːn/ | auf dem Bildschirm | It was perhaps the first time we had seen a man take his clothes off **on screen**. |

Truth or tabloid? (p. 104–106)

flattering (adj) (TS)	/ˈflætərɪŋ/	schmeichelhaft	The photos they printed of her weren't very **flattering**.
mainstream (adj)	/ˈmeɪnstriːm/	der Mitte	The story appeared in a **mainstream** newspaper.
checkout (n)	/ˈtʃekaʊt/	Kasse	People often recognise me at supermarket **checkouts**.
circulation (n)	/ˌsɜːkjəˈleɪʃn/	Auflage	Newspapers print scandal to increase **circulation**.
disregard (n) (TS)	/ˌdɪsrɪˈɡɑːd/	Geringschätzung	The tabloids have a total **disregard** for truth or accuracy.
feature (n) (TS)	/ˈfiːtʃə(r)/	Leitartikel	They love to write **feature**s about big stars.
gutter-press (n) (TS)	/ˈɡʌtəˌpres/	Sensationspresse	I'm sick of the **gutter-press** making up stories.
headline (n)	/ˈhedlaɪn/	Schlagzeile	Sensational **headline**s sell papers.
inaccuracy (n)	/ɪnˈækjərəsɪ/	Ungenauigkeit	The editor admitted there were some **inaccuracies** in the story.
news-stand (n)	/ˈnjuːztænd/	Kiosk	Bronstein and Stone saw on the **news-stand**s that they had broken up.
restriction (n) (TS)	/rɪˈstrɪkʃn/	Einschränkung	Do you think **restriction**s should be placed on the press?
scandal (n)	/ˈskændl/	Skandal	Do you enjoy reading celebrity **scandal**s?
make up (phr v)	/meɪk ˈʌp/	erfinden	The story was totally **made up**.
splash across (phr v) (TS)	/ˌsplæʃ əˈkrɒs/	groß rausbringen	The headline was **splashed across** the front page of the newspaper.
beg (v) (TS)	/beɡ/	anflehen	She used to **beg** us to write features about her.
be under fire (TS)	/biː ˌʌndə ˈfaɪə(r)/	im Kreuzfeuer der Kritik liegen	The tabloid press **is under fire** yet again.
in the news	/ˌɪn ðə ˈnjuːz/	in den Nachrichten	What scandals are **in the news** at the moment?
(There's) no smoke without fire. (TS)	/(ðeəz) nəʊ ˌsməʊk wɪðaʊt ˈfaɪə(r)/	Kein Rauch ohne Feuer.	People are bound to deny these stories but **there's no smoke without fire,** that's what I say.
on the world stage	/ɒn ðə ˌwɜːld ˈsteɪdʒ/	auf der Weltbühne	**On the world stage**, I'm Mr Sharon Stone.
the root of the problem (TS)	/ðə ˌruːt əv ðə ˈprɒbləm/	die Ursache des Problems	I think we need to address **the root of the problem**.
a straight answer	/ə ˌstreɪt ˈɑːnsə(r)/	eine klare Antwort	Why can politicians never give **a straight answer**.
take a year off	/teɪk ə ˌjɪər ˈɒf/	ein Jahr frei nehmen	I'd love to **take a year off** to travel.
The thing I like/hate about …	/ðə ˌθɪŋ aɪ ˈlaɪk/ˈheɪt əˌbaʊt/	Was mir an … gefällt/missfällt …	**The thing I like about** Florida is the climate.
What I find annoying/difficult is …	/wɒt aɪ faɪnd əˈnɔɪɪŋ/ˈdɪfɪkəlt ɪz/	Was ich ärgerlich/schwierig finde	**What I find annoying** is that a lot of the stories aren't true.
What I love/hate about …	/wɒt aɪ ˈlʌv/ˈheɪt əˌbaʊt/	Was ich an … mag/nicht mag …	**What I hate about** my job is having to work weekends.

The Blair Witch Project (p. 107–108)

absolute (adj)	/ˈæbsəluːt/	absolut	He thought the film was **absolute** rubbish.
apprehensive (adj)	/ˌæprɪˈhensɪv/	voll gespannter Erwartung	I felt quite **apprehensive** before seeing the film.
hand-held (adj)	/ˈhændheld/	Hand-	The actors were sent into the woods with **hand-held** cameras.

over-hyped (adj) (TS)	/ˌəʊvəˈhaɪpt/	aufgeblasen	The film was **over-hyped** nonsense.
uneasy (adj)	/ʌnˈiːzɪ/	unruhig	I must admit, I feel a little **uneasy**.
unexplained (adj)	/ˌʌnɪkˈspleɪnd/	unerklärlich	The film is based on a series of **unexplained** disappearances.
unseen (adj)	/ʌnˈsiːn/	unsichtbar	They seemed to have been terrorised by something **unseen**.
utter (adj)	/ˈʌtə(r)/	vollkommen	What a load of **utter** rubbish!
camera angles (n pl) (TS)	/ˈkæmrə ˌæŋglz/	Kameraperspektive	The **camera angle**s made me feel sick.
footage (n)	/ˈfʊtɪdʒ/	Filmbilder	The Blair Witch Project is a compilation of the **footage** they took.
letdown (n)	/ˈletdaʊn/	Enttäuschung	I thought it was a massive **letdown**.
motion sickness (n) (Am E) (TS)	/ˌməʊʃn ˈsɪknəs/	Fahrtkrankheit	Don't go to see this film if you suffer from **motion sickness**!
outcome (n)	/ˈaʊtkʌm/	Resultat	The **outcome** of all the hype is that The Blair Witch Project is one of the most profitable films of all time.
ploy (n)	/plɔɪ/	Trick	The decision to release the film in only a few cinemas was a clever marketing **ploy**.
rations (n pl)	/ˈræʃənz/	Zuteilungen	The actors were given minimal **rations** each day.
screening (n)	/ˈskriːnɪŋ/	Filmvorstellung	Six months before the first **screening**, the directors set up a website.
script (n)	/skrɪpt/	Drehbuch	The actors worked without a **script**.
set-up (n)	/ˈsetʌp/	Zweck	The actors understood the general **'set-up'** of the story well.
shoot (v)	/ʃuːt/	filmen	The film was **shot** in eight days.
unfold (v)	/ʌnˈfəʊld/	sich entwickeln	The story **unfolds** in a totally believable way.
update (v)	/ʌpˈdeɪt/	aktualisieren	The website was **updated** on a weekly basis.
bored stiff	/bɔːd ˈstɪf/	zu Tode gelangweilt	Some of the audience said they were **bored stiff**.
come up with an idea	/kʌm ʌp wɪð ən aɪˈdɪə/	auf eine Idee kommen	The directors **came up with the idea** of a legend about unexplained disappearances.
frightened to death	/fraɪtənd təˈdeθ/	Todesängste ausstehen	We expected to be **frightened to death**.
go wild/mad	/gəʊ ˈwʊɪld/ˈmæd/	verrückt werden	The media **went mad** when the film was released.

42

Unit 12

Could do better (p. 109–110)

compulsory (adj)	/kəmˈpʌlsərɪ/	verpflichtend	Do you think military service should be **compulsory**?
deaf (adj) (TS)	/def/	taub	He used to shout at us as if we were **deaf**.
imbecilic (adj) (TS)	/ˌɪmbəˈsɪlɪk/	einfältig	Take that **imbecilic** grin off your face!
vicious (adj) (TS)	/ˈvɪʃəs/	gemein, gehässig	My old French teacher could be absolutely **vicious**.
bun (n) (TS)	/bʌn/	Dutt	She had blond hair tied in a tight **bun**.
catchphrase (n) (TS)	/ˈkætʃfreɪz/	Schlagwort	'You are an imbecile' was her **catchphrase**.
compact mirror (n) (TS)	/ˈkɒmpækt ˌmɪrə(r)/	Taschenspiegel	She carried a **compact mirror** and lipstick in her handbag.
detention (n)	/dɪˈtenʃn/	nachsitzen	Do you get **detention** at your school?

grin (n) (TS)	/grɪn/	Grinsen	Take that stupid **grin** off your face!
lad (n)	/læd/	Junge	He just wanted to play with the other **lad**s.
retirement (n) (TS)	/rɪ'taɪəmənt/	Ruhestand	She must have been near to **retirement**.
score (n) (TS)	/skɔ:(r)/	Ergebnis	The only thing that's funny is your **score** in the French exam last year!
get up to (phr v)	/get ˈʌp tə/	im Schilde führen	He did the sort of stuff you'd expect a 14-year-old to **get up to**.
tell off (phr v)	/ˌtel ˈɒf/	zurechtweisen	The rest of the class would be laughing and get **told off**.
abolish (v)	/ə'bɒlɪʃ/	abschaffen	Should compulsory military service be **abolished**?
giggle (v) (TS)	/'gɪgl/	kichern	When she mentioned Marcel everyone used to **giggle**.
pursue (v)	/pə'sju:/	verfolgen	After leaving Take That he decided to **pursue** a solo career.
twitch (v) (TS)	/twɪtʃ/	zucken	Mr Tucker's eye used to **twitch** when he got angry.
be more concerned with	/bɪ ˌmɔ: kən'sɜ:nd wɪð/	mehr Interesse haben an	He **was more concerned with** playing with the lads than with saying goodbye to his mum.
get caught	/get ˈkɔ:t/	ertappt werden	He did a lot of naughty things but never **got caught**.
in a funny sort of way (TS)	/ɪn ə ˌfʌnɪ sɔ:t əv ˈweɪ/	auf komische Art und Weise	I enjoyed her lessons **in a funny sort of way**.
in that ...	/'ɪn ðæt/	darin, dass ...	He was lucky **in that** he never got caught.
knock some sense into sb	/nɒk sʌm ˈsens ɪntə sʌmbədi/	jmd. zur Vernunft bringen	The army would **knock some sense into you**.
reduce sb to tears	/rɪˌdju:s sʌmbədi tə 'tɪəz/	jmd. zum Weinen bringen	She **reduced me to tears** on many occasions.
you lot (TS)	/'ju: ˌlɒt/	ihr alle	My generation never had the opportunities that **you lot** have.
You'll never amount to much.	/ju:l ˌnevə(r) əmaʊnt tə 'mʌtʃ/	Du wirst es nicht weit bringen.	You imbecile! **You'll never amount to much**.

Look at us now!/Listening (p. 111–112)

mediocre (adj)	/ˌmi:dɪˈəʊkə(r)/	mittelmäßig	Ann's teachers thought she was a **mediocre** student.
accounts (n pl)	/ə'kaʊnts/	finanzielle Verwaltung	She does all her own **accounts**.
acting school (n)	/'æktɪŋ ˌsku:l/	Schauspielschule	Henry went to **acting school**.
birth-rate (n)	/'bɜ:θreɪt/	Geburtenrate	Is the **birth-rate** decreasing in your country?
boarding school (n)	/'bɔ:dɪŋ ˌsku:l/	Internat	A **boarding school** is one where students can live during term-time.
catering company (n)	/'keɪtərɪŋ ˌkʌmpəni/	Catering-Unternehmen	A **catering company** provides food and drinks for special occasions.
degree (n)	/dɪ'gri:/	Titel	Do you think it's important to get a university **degree**?
fate (n)	/feɪt/	Schicksal	I suppose it was **fate** that I ended up at acting school.
further education (n)	/ˌfɜ:ðə(r) ˌedʒə'keɪʃn/	weiterführende Schule	Do you want to go on to **further education**?
grant (n)	/grɑ:nt/	Stipendium, Ausbildungs-förderungsbeihilfe	Nowadays it's not always easy for students to get **grant**s.
nun (n)	/nʌn/	Nonne	Ann's boarding school was run by **nun**s.
report (n)	/rɪ'pɔ:t/	Zeugnis	Do you usually get a good school **report**?
start off (phr v)	/ˌstɑ:t ˈɒf/	anfangen	How did Romy **start off**?
try out (phr v) (TS)	/ˌtraɪ ˈaʊt/	versuchen	Saffron wants to **try out** the music business.
cater (v)	/ˈkeɪtə(r)/	mit Mahlzeiten versorgen	We **cater** mainly for conferences.

enrol (v)	/enˈrəʊl/	sich anmelden	Have you ever **enrolled** for an evening course?
raise (v)	/reɪz/	aufziehen	Did Ann want to get married and **raise** a family?
reckon (v)	/ˈrekən/	annehmen	She **reckons** she's going to have a career as a pop star.
as they say	/əz ðeɪ ˈseɪ/	wie gesagt	The rest is history, **as they say**.
be best suited to	/bɪ ˌbest ˈsuːtəd tə/	am besten geeignet sein für	They told her she would **be best suited to** family life.
by heart	/ˌbaɪ ˈhɑːt/	auswendig	There are some things you have to learn **by heart**.
come to one's senses	/ˌkʌm tə wʌnz ˈsensɪz/	zur Besinnung kommen	We just hope she'll **come to her senses** and realize her mistake.
follow in sb's footsteps	/ˌfɒləʊ ɪn sʌmbədɪz ˈfʊtsteps/	in jmd. Fußstapfen treten	When it comes to a career, do you intend to **follow in your parents' footsteps**?
get sth out of one's system	/ˌget sʌmθɪŋ ˌaʊt əv wʌnz ˈsɪstəm/	etwas verarbeiten	Sometimes you have to let people **get things out of their system**.
A bit of ... goes a long way!	/ə ˌbɪt əv ... gəʊz ə ˌlɒŋ ˈweɪ/	Ein kleines Bisschen ... hilft schon viel.	Believe me, **a bit of** motivation **goes a long way**!
have sth behind you	/ˌhæv sʌmθɪŋ bɪˈhaɪnd jə/	etw. in der Hinterhand haben	It's important to **have qualifications behind you**.
I see little point in ...	/aɪ siː ˌlɪtl ˈpɔɪnt ɪn .../	Es hat wenig Sinn, ...	**I see little point in** entering her for the exam.
judging by ...	/ˈdʒʌdʒɪŋ ˌbaɪ/	nach ... zu urteilen	**Judging by** her low marks, I don't think she's likely to pass.
It's up to you/her/him etc	/ɪts ˌʌp tə ˈjuː/ˈhɜː/ˈhɪm/	Es ist seine/ihre Sache, ...	**It's up to her** to make things work.
make it	/ˈmeɪk ɪt/	erfolgreich sein	Do you think she'll **make it** in the pop world?
not make much of an impression	/ˌnɒt meɪk ˌmʌtʃ əv ən ɪmˈpreʃn/	keinen guten Eindruck machen	Ann **didn't make much of an impression** at school.
The rest is history.	/ðə ˌrest ɪz ˈhɪstrɪ/	Der Rest ist Geschichte.	Henry went to acting school and **the rest is history**.
have a taste of freedom	/ə ˌteɪst əv ˈfriːdəm/	die Freiheit schmecken	It's difficult to go back to living at home when you've **had a taste of freedom**.

44

Close up (p. 113–114)

posh (adj)	/pɒʃ/	schick	Have you ever stayed in a **posh** hotel?
fabulously (adv)	/ˈfæbjələslɪ/	fabelhaft	One day I'm going to be **fabulously** rich.
lead singer (n)	/ˌliːd ˈsɪŋə(r)/	Leadsänger	Saffron is **lead singer** in a band.
live off (phr v)	/ˈlɪv ˌɒf/	leben von	Do you think you'll be able to **live off** your music career?
by this time next year	/baɪ ˌðɪs taɪm ˌnekst ˈjɪə(r)/	nächstes Jahr um diese Zeit	**By this time next year** we'll have a record in the charts.
five years from now	/ˌfaɪv jɪəz frəm ˈnaʊ/	in 5 Jahren	I wonder what I'll be doing **five years from now**.
I bet you	/aɪ ˈbet juː/	Wetten, dass	**I bet you** we'll have a record in the charts soon.
just as soon as	/dʒʌst əz ˈsuːn əz/	sobald	**Just as soon as** I've left school I want to move to London.
the minute she's ...	/ðə ˈmɪnɪt ʃiːz/	unmittelbar, nachdem sie	She wants to get a manager **the minute she's** taken her last exam.
No way.	/ˌnəʊ ˈweɪ/	Auf keinen Fall.	'Are you going to continue living at home?' **'No way.'**
not as such	/ˌnɒt əz ˈsʌtʃ/	an sich nicht	'Have you got a contract then?' 'Er, **not as such**.'
not be too bothered about	/ˌnɒt bɪ tuː ˈbɒðəd əˌbaʊt/	sich nicht sehr um etwas kümmern	I'm **not too bothered about** my exam results.
where it all happens	/ˌweə(r) ɪt ɔːl ˈhæpənz/	wo sich alles Wichtige abspielt	London is **where it all happens** in the music industry.

Backpacking (p. 115–116)

filthy (adj)	/ˈfɪlθɪ/	schmutzig	The room was absolutely **filthy**.
mind-blowing (adj)	/ˈmaɪndˌbləʊɪŋ/	atemberaubend	The scenery was beautiful – just **mind-blowing**.
raging (adj)	/ˈreɪdʒɪŋ/	hoch, wütend	He had to stay in bed with a **raging** fever.
smelly (adj)	/ˈsmelɪ/	stinkend	He fell into a **smelly** latrine.
stinking (adj)	/ˈstɪŋkɪŋ/	stinkend	It was a horrible **stinking** toilet!
tough (adj)	/tʌf/	schwierig	Trekking in the Himalayas was one of the **toughest** things I've ever done.
ant (n)	/ænt/	Ameise	**Ants** were climbing up the walls.
backpacking (n)	/ˈbækˌpækɪŋ/	Ferien mit dem Rucksack	Students often go **backpacking** in their summer holidays.
blade (n)	/bleɪd/	Blatt eines Ventilators	He was hit on the head by one of the **blade**s.
bungee jump (n)	/ˈbʌndʒɪ ˌdʒʌmp/	Bungeejumping	Have you ever done a **bungee jump**?
bunk bed (n)	/ˈbʌŋk ˌbed/	Stockbett	Have you ever slept in a **bunk bed**?
buzz (n)	/bʌz/	Aufregung	With the holidays approaching, there's a real **buzz** around.
ceiling fan (n)	/ˈsiːlɪŋ ˌfæn/	Ventilator an der Zimmerdecke	**Ceiling fan**s are essential in a hot climate.
diarrhoea (n)	/ˌdaɪəˈrɪə/	Durchfall	I got **diarrhoea** when I was in India.
gunfire (n)	/ˈgʌn ˌfaɪə(r)/	Gewehrschüsse	We heard the sound of **gunfire** in the distance.
lifetime (n)	/ˈlaɪftaɪm/	ein Leben lang	I stayed in bed for what felt like a **lifetime**.
lobster (n)	/ˈlɒbstə(r)/	Hummer	The ants were as big as **lobster**s.
rite of passage (n)	/ˌraɪt əv ˈpæsɪdʒ/	Ritual des Erwachsenwerdens	These adventures mark **rite of passage** from child to adult.
skull (n)	/skʌl/	Schädel	He was hit on the **skull** by one of the fan blades.
stitch (n)	/stɪtʃ/	Stich	He had five **stitch**es in his skull.
tale (n)	/teɪl/	Erzählung	Students sometimes exaggerate their **tale**s.
thigh (n)	/θaɪ/	Hüfte	Ants had bitten my **thigh**.
black out (phr v)	/ˌblæk ˈaʊt/	ohnmächtig werden	I **blacked out** and fell on the ground.
blow up (phr v)	/ˌbləʊ ˈʌp/	anschwellen	Suddenly a storm **blew up**.
swell up (phr v)	/ˌswel ˈʌp/	anschwellen	His thigh had **swollen up** like a balloon.
bash (v)	/bæʃ/	erschlagen	I **bashed** the ant with my shoe.
dent (v)	/dent/	verbeulen	She reversed into a wall and **dented** the car.
dodge (v)	/dɒdʒ/	ausweichen	We had to **dodge** gunfire.
embellish (v)	/ɪmˈbelɪʃ/	beschönigen	People like **embellishing** stories.
faint (v)	/feɪnt/	umfallen	I was in so much pain I **fainted**.
spot (v)	/spɒt/	entdecken	I suddenly **spotted** an ant on the ceiling.
across the land	/əˌkrɒs ðə ˈlænd/	überall im Land	**Across the land** students are busy planning foreign trips.
be at the end of one's tether	/bi: ət ðɪ ˌend əv wʌnz ˈteðə(r)/	am Ende seiner Kräfte sein	She was in so much pain she was **at the end of her tether**.
be in pain	/bi: ɪn ˈpeɪn/	Schmerzen haben	What's wrong? **Are** you **in pain**?

be on (one's) last legs	/biː ɒn (wʌnz) ˌlɑːst ˈlegz/	sich kaum mehr auf den Beinen halten können	We'd been walking all day and I **was on my last legs**.
be swarming with	/bɪ ˈswɔːmɪŋ ˌwɪð/	wimmeln von	The room **was swarming with** ants.
at death's door	/ˌdeθs ˈdɔː/	an der Schwelle des Todes	He looked as if he was **at death's door**.
feel like death	/ˌfiːl laɪk ˈdeθ/	sich wie tot fühlen	She lay in bed **feeling like death**.
get hold of	/get ˈhəʊld əv/	etwas auftreiben	Finally we managed to **get hold of** some antibiotics.
go berserk	/ˌgəʊ bəˈzɜːk/	rasend werden	He was **going berserk** trying to kill the ants.
go out of one's mind	/ˌgəʊ ˌaʊt əv wʌnz ˈmaɪnd/	verrückt werden	She was **going out of her mind** with worry.
It turned out that ...	/ɪt tɜːnd ˈaʊt ðət .../	Es stellte sich heraus, dass ...	**It turned out that** my skull had been dented.
take sth with a pinch of salt	/ˌteɪk sʌmθɪŋ wɪð ə ˌpɪntʃ əv ˈsɒlt/	etwas nicht ganz wörtlich nehmen	You should **take everything he says with a pinch of salt**.
wracked with pain	/ˌrækt wɪð ˈpeɪn/	schmerzverzerrt	She lay on the floor, **wracked with pain**.

Job hunting (p. 117–118)

interpersonal skills (n pl)	/ˌɪntəpɜːsənl ˈskɪlz/	zwischenmenschliche Fähigkeiten	She's good at dealing with people and has excellent **interpersonal** skills.
self-assured (adj)	/ˌselfəˈʃɔːd/	selbstsicher	Being **self-assured** is a good thing but being over-confident isn't.
unconventional (adj)	/ˌʌnkənˈvenʃənl/	unkonventionell	Ben's appearance is **unconventional** but interesting.
single-handed (adv)	/ˌsɪŋglˈhændəd/	im Alleingang	He ran the restaurant **single-handed**.
challenge (n)	/ˈtʃælɪndʒ/	Herausforderung	Are you the sort of person who likes a **challenge**?
character reference (n)	/ˈkærəktə ˌrefrəns/	Referenz	Ben asked Pete to write him a **character reference**.
child-minding (n)	/ˈtʃaɪldˌmaɪndɪŋ/	Babysitten	Have you ever done any **child-minding**?
commitment (n)	/kəˈmɪtmənt/	Engagement	If he's interested in a job he'll give total **commitment** to it.
device (n)	/dɪˈvaɪs/	Element, Mittel	Don't use too many decorative **device**s on a CV.
font (n)	/fɒnt/	Schriftart	There are lots of different types of **font** including italic, bold and roman.
food poisoning (n) (TS)	/ˈfuːd ˌpɔɪzənɪŋ/	Lebensmittelvergiftung	They're off work with **food poisoning**.
referee (n)	/ˌrefəˈriː/	jmd., der als Referenz dient	When you apply for a job you usually need two **referee**s to write references for you.
retail trade (n)	/ˈriːteɪl ˌtreɪd/	Einzelhandel	Have you ever worked in the **retail trade**?
show-off (n)	/ˈʃəʊɒf/	Angeber	He can be a bit of a **show-off** at times.
summer camp (n) (TS)	/ˈsʌmə ˌkæmp/	Freizeitlager im Sommer	He's applied for a job at a children's **summer camp**.
tip (n)	/tɪp/	Hinweis	Follow these useful **tip**s when writing your CV.
trouble-maker (n)	/ˈtrʌblˌmeɪkə(r)/	Unruhestifter	A **trouble-maker** causes problems for people.
typing (n)	/ˈtaɪpɪŋ/	Tippen	You need a **typing** speed of 60 words per minute for the job.
word-processing (n)	/ˈwɜːdˈprəʊsesɪŋ/	Textverarbeitung	**Word-processing** is a useful skill.
relate to (phr v)	/rɪˈleɪt tə/	gut umgehen können mit	He **relates** well **to** children.
as regards	/əz rɪˈgɑːdz/	in Bezug auf	**As regards** working with children, I'm sure he'd be excellent at it.
have no hesitation in doing sth	/hæv ˌnəʊ ˌhezɪteɪʃn ɪn ˈduːɪŋ sʌmθɪŋ/	nicht zögen, etwas zu tun	**I have no hesitation in recommending** him for the job.

keep it simple	/ˌkiːp ɪt ˈsɪmpl/	mach es einfach	Don't give too many details – try to **keep it simple**.
out of order (TS)	/ˌaʊt əv ˈɔːdə(r)/	defekt	Writing a letter? Is your phone **out of order**?
provided (that)	/prəˈvaɪdɪd (ðət)/	vorausgesetzt, dass	**Provided that** he's interested in the job, he'll show total commitment to it.

Unit 13

Home/Close up (p. 120–123)

calming (adj) (TS)	/ˈkɑːmɪŋ/	beruhigend	There's nothing very **calming** about this room.
cluttered (adj) (TS)	/ˈklʌtəd/	vollgestopft	This room is really **cluttered** – every surface is covered.
high-rise (adj)	/ˈhaɪ ˌraɪz/	Hoch-	We live on the fifth floor of a **high-rise** building.
warm-hearted (adj) (TS)	/ˌwɔːmˈhɑːtəd/	warmherzig	Bright colours suggest a person who is **warm-hearted**.
banisters (n)	/ˈbænɪstəz/	Geländer	She held on to the **banisters** as she went up the stairs.
blinds (n pl)	/blaɪndz/	Jalousien	Pull the **blinds** down to keep out the sun.
bolt (n)	/bəʊlt/	Riegel	He slid the **bolt** across the door to fasten it.
cellar (n)	/ˈselə(r)/	Keller	People often use **cellar**s for storing things.
clue (n) (TS)	/kluː/	Hinweis	There aren't many **clues** about the type of person who lives here.
context (n) (TS)	/ˈkɒntekst/	Beziehung	He has little time to socialise, except in a working **context**.
double glazing (n)	/ˌdʌbl ˈɡleɪzɪŋ/	Doppelverglasung	**Double glazing** helps to keep rooms warmer.
fireplace (n)	/ˈfaɪəpleɪs/	(offener) Kamin	A fire was burning in the **fireplace**.
floorboards (n pl)	/ˈflɔːbɔːdz/	Dielen	There were wooden **floorboards** in all the bedrooms.
knocker (n)	/ˈnɒkə(r)/	Klopfer	She knocked on the door using the brass door **knocker**.
latch (n)	/lætʃ/	Klinke	She heard the sound of someone lifting the **latch**.
letterbox (n)	/ˈletəbɒks/	Briefkasten	She lifted the **letterbox** and peered inside the apartment.
loft (n)	/lɒft/	Dachboden	We use the **loft** for storing things.
mantelpiece (n)	/ˈmæntlpiːs/	Kamin	The **mantelpiece** was covered in photos of the family.
ornament (n) (TS)	/ˈɔːnəmənt/	Dekoration	Do you have a lot of **ornaments** in your house?
party animal (n)	/ˈpɑːti ˌænɪml/	Partylöwe	A **party animal** is someone who loves going to parties.
pastel (n) (TS)	/ˈpæstl/	Pastellfarbe	There are loads of bright colours but hardly any **pastels**.
power point (n)	/ˈpaʊə ˌpɔɪnt/	Steckdose	A **power point** is a place where you can plug in an electrical appliance.
radiator (n)	/ˈreɪdiˌeɪtə(r)/	Heizkörper	They stood near the **radiator** trying to keep warm.
rug (n)	/rʌɡ/	Teppich	There was a beautiful oriental **rug** on the floor.
shutters (n pl)	/ˈʃʌtəz/	Fensterläden	Houses in the UK don't have **shutters**.
staircase (n)	/ˈsteəkeɪs/	Treppe	He climbed slowly up the **staircase**.
study (n)	/ˈstʌdi/	Arbeitszimmer	Dad's working in the **study**.
stuff (n)	/stʌf/	Kram	The room's cluttered with too much **stuff**.

terraced house (n)	/ˌterəst 'haʊs/	Reihenhaus	A **terraced house** is a house in a row of houses that are joined together.
tile (n)	/taɪl/	Fliese	The bathroom walls are covered in **tiles**.
entertain (v) (TS)	/ˌentə'teɪn/	Gäste haben	We don't **entertain** much at home.
at short notice	/ət ʃɔːt 'nəʊtɪs/	kurzfristig	You have to be prepared to travel to see clients **at short notice**.
at the top of one's lungs	/ət ðə ˌtɒp əv wʌnz 'lʌŋz/	aus Leibeskräften	Home is where I can scream **at the top of my lungs** and no one minds.
bring sb down to earth (TS)	/brɪŋ sʌmbədi daʊn tu: 'ɜːθ/	jmd. auf den Boden der Tatschen zurückholen	More green would help to **bring** this person **down to earth**.
far too much	/fɑ: tu: 'mʌtʃ/	viel zuviel	There's **far too much stuff** in the room.
nine times out of ten (TS)	/ˌnaɪn taɪmz ˌaʊt əv 'ten/	in neun von zehn Fällen	**Nine times out of ten**, cushions don't actually make seats more comfortable.
on display (TS)	/ɒn dɪ'spleɪ/	zur Schau gestellt	There aren't many personal objects **on display**.
pack one's bags	/pæk wʌnz 'bægz/	sich aus dem Staub machen	We were just told to **pack our bags** and leave.
piles of (TS)	/'paɪlz əv/	Stapel von	There are **piles of** cushions everywhere.
two/three/four-bedroomed	/ˌtu:/ˌθri:/ˌfɔ: 'bedru:md/	Zwei-/Drei-/Vierzimmer-	We live in a **three-bedroomed** house.
two/three/four-storey	/ˌtu:/ˌθri:/ˌfɔ: 'stɔːri/	mit 2/3/4 Stockwerken	I work in a **five-storey** building.
you can tell (TS)	/ju: kən 'tel/	wie man sieht	A woman lives here, **you can tell**.

Rise and shine/Feng Shui (p. 124–125)

bleary-eyed (adj)	/'blɪəriˌaɪd/	mit schläfrigem Blick	He made his way, **bleary-eyed**, to the breakfast table.
ceramic (adj)	/sə'ræmɪk/	Keramik-	It's a good idea to choose **ceramic** tiles for your floors.
clutter-free (adj)	/'klʌtəfri:/	ohne Krempel	A **clutter-free** environment is very important.
fizzy (adj)	/'fɪzi/	kohlensäurehaltig	Do you like **fizzy** drinks?
uplifting (adj)	/ʌp'lɪftɪŋ/	aufmunternd	Feng Shui is basically the art of creating an **uplifting** environment.
seaweed (n) (TS)	/'si:wi:d/	Seegras	Miso soup consists of vegetables, **seaweed** and tofu.
transition (n)	/træn'zɪʃn/	Übergang	Morning marks the **transition** from sleeping to waking.
work surface (n)	/'wɜːk ˌsɜːfɪs/	Arbeitsplatz	**Work-surfaces** should be clutter-free.
worktop (n)	/'wɜːktɒp/	Arbeitsplatte	Wooden **worktop**s and tables allow energy to flow through the room.
guarantee (v)	/gærən'ti:/	garantieren	I **guarantee** that this will make you feel better.
re-do (v)	/ˌriː'du:/	herrichten	We're thinking of **re-doing** the kitchen.
rumble (v)	/'rʌmblɪŋ/	knurren	Your stomach's **rumbling**. Are you hungry?
skip (v)	/skɪp/	auslassen	It's definitely not a good idea to **skip** breakfast.
east/west/south/north-facing	/'i:st/'west/'saʊθ/'nɔːθˌfeɪsɪŋ/	auf der Ost-/West-/Süd-/Nordseite	Try to eat breakfast in an **east-facing** room.
failing that	/ˌfeɪlɪŋ 'ðæt/	mangels dessen	Try to use plants and fresh flowers. **Failing that**, inspire yourself with a picture on the wall.
get off on the wrong foot	/get ˌɒf ɒn ðə ˌrɒŋ 'fʊt/	mit dem falschen Fuß aufstehen	If you **get off on the wrong foot**, things will probably continue to get worse.
go from bad to worse	/gəʊ frəm ˌbæd tə'wɜːs/	immer schlimmer werden	During the rest of the day things just **went from bad to worse**.
make or break	/ˌmeɪk ɔː 'breɪk/	etw. steht oder fällt mit	According to Simon Brown, the right breakfast can **make or break** your day.
make one's way	/ˌmeɪk wʌnz 'weɪ/	sich bewegen	She **made her way** slowly downstairs.
on an empty stomach	/ɒn ən ˌempti 'stʌmək/	mit leerem Magen	Don't go to work **on an empty stomach**.

The Freedom Ship/Close up (p. 126–127)

crime-free (adj)	/ˈkraɪmfriː/	ohme Kriminalität	The aim is to ensure a **crime-free** environment.
hurricane-force (adj)	/ˌhʌrɪkənˈfɔːs/	mit Orkanstärke	The ship will be designed to resist **hurricane-force** winds.
perpetual (adj)	/pəˈpetʃʊəl/	ewig	The ship's route will keep residents in **perpetual** sunshine.
proposed (adj)	/prəˈpəʊzd/	geplant	The **proposed** ship is so large it will have to be built at sea.
self-financing (adj)	/ˌselfˈfaɪnænsɪŋ/	sich selbst finanzierend	It is hoped that the project will be **self-financing**.
fully (adv)	/ˈfʊlɪ/	vollkommen	The project is intended to be **fully** self-financing.
airstrip (n)	/ˈeəstrɪp/	Landebahn	An **airstrip** will run along the top of the ship.
barbed wire (n)	/ˌbɑːbd ˈwaɪə(r)/	Stacheldraht	The wall was constructed of concrete and **barbed wire**.
cycle (n)	/ˈsaɪkl/	Zeitraum	The ship will circle the globe in two-year **cycles**.
deposit (n)	/dɪˈpɒzɪt/	Anzahlung	**Deposits** have already been placed for 100 homes.
diner (n)	/ˈdaɪnə(r)/	speisender Gast	**Diners** in the restaurants will have a wide choice of food.
docking (n)	/ˈdɒkɪŋ/	Ankerplatz	**Docking** space for yachts and hydrofoils will be provided.
excise duty (n)	/ˈeksaɪz ˌdjuːtɪ/	Verbrauchssteuer	Passengers will not pay tax or **excise duty**.
harbour (n)	/ˈhɑːbə(r)/	Hafen	A **harbour** will be provided for ferries and private yachts.
hydrofoil (n)	/ˈhaɪdrəfɔɪl/	Tragflügelboot	**Hydrofoils** travel at high speeds across the surface of the water.
mooring (n)	/ˈmɔːrɪŋ/	Liegeplatz	**Mooring** for yachts and ferries will be available in the harbour.
perk (n)	/pɜːk/	Vorteil	One of the **perks** for passengers is not having to pay tax.
runway (n)	/ˈrʌnweɪ/	Start-/Landebahn	A 3,800-foot **runway** will be situated along the top deck of the ship.
scepticism (n)	/ˈskeptɪsɪzm/	Skepsis	Dr Brown's comments show a certain **scepticism**.
scrap (n)	/skræp/	Altmaterial	Waste that cannot be burnt will be sold for **scrap**.
sewage (n)	/ˈsuːɪdʒ/	Abwasser	**Sewage** will be incinerated in electric toilets.
tax haven (n)	/ˈtæks ˌheɪvn/	Steuerparadies	A **tax haven** is a place where you do not have to pay any tax.
upkeep (n)	/ˈʌpkiːp/	(Lebenshaltungs-)Kosten	Passengers will have to pay money every month towards the ship's **upkeep**.
vessel (n)	/ˈvesl/	Fahrzeug	The enormous **vessel** will be built by Engineering Solutions.
waterfall (n)	/ˈwɔːtəfɔːl/	Wasserfall	They plan to build parks with trees and **waterfalls**.
cater for (phr v)	/ˈkeɪtə fə/	ausgerichtet sein auf	The runway will **cater for** both helicopters and commercial aircraft.
speed up (phr v)	/ˌspiːd ˈʌp/	beschleunigen	Work has been **speeded up** by the use of new technology.
throw together (phr v)	/ˌθrəʊ təˈgeðə(r)/	zusammenbringen	I can't imagine anything worse than being **thrown together** with 65,000 other people.
anchor (v)	/ˈæŋkə(r)/	vor Anker liegen	Three-quarters of the time, the ship will be **anchored** close to big cities.
arouse (v)	/əˈraʊz/	wecken	Early buyers are being offered a 35% discount to **arouse** interest.
circumnavigate (v)	/ˌsɜːkəmˈnævɪgeɪt/	(um die Welt) navigieren	It will **circumnavigate** the globe once every two years.
cruise (v)	/kruːz/	befahren	How long will it take the ship to **cruise** the world?
dismantle (v)	/dɪsˈmæntl/	abbrechen	The wall was **dismantled** as quickly as it was erected.
displace (v)	/dɪsˈpleɪs/	versetzen	A 25-metre wave would only **displace** the ship by 2 centimetres.

erect (v)	/ɪˈrekt/	bauen	The Berlin Wall was **erected** in 1961.
handle (v)	/ˈhændl/	abwickeln	The airport will be capable of **handling** both commercial and private aircraft.
incinerate (v)	/ɪnˈsɪnəreɪt/	verbrennen	Sewage will be **incinerated** in electric toilets.
launch (v)	/lɔːntʃ/	zu Wasser lassen	When was the Titanic **launched**?
screen (v)	/skriːn/	überprüfen, durchleuchten	All passengers will be **screened** to ensure a crime-free environment.
withstand (v)	/wɪðˈstænd/	standhalten	The ship will be designed to **withstand** storms and hurricanes.
at the rear	/ət ðə ˈrɪə(r)/	auf der Rückseite	Power will be provided by 100 engines **at the rear**.
get away from it all	/get əˌweɪ frəm ɪt ˈɔːl/	einen Tapetenwechsel haben	We all need to **get away from it all** occasionally.
be greeted with	/bɪ ˈgriːtəd ˌwɪð/	begegnen mit	The plans have **been greeted with** a mixture or surprise and scepticism.
the high seas	/ðə ˌhaɪ ˈsiːz/	offene See	Would you like to live on the Freedom Ship and cruise **the high seas**?
in transit	/ɪn ˈtrænzɪt/	unterwegs	The ship will spend a quarter of its time **in transit**.
miss the point	/ˌmɪs ðə ˈpɔɪnt/	das Wesentliche nicht verstehen	People who buy an apartment on the ship may be **missing the point**.
on board	/ɒn ˈbɔːd/	an Bord	Residents will be able to work **on board**.
think big	/ˌθɪŋk ˈbɪg/	große Pläne haben	Dr Brown thinks that the company shouldn't **think** so **big**.

Home page (p. 129–130)

acclaimed (adj)	/əˈkleɪmd/	gefeiert	The **acclaimed** series is watched regularly by over 9 million viewers.
award-winning (adj)	/əwɔːd wɪnɪŋ/	preisgekrönt	Visit our **award-winning** website.
hazardous (adj)	/ˈhæzədəs/	gefährlich	Click here to find out more about what types of activity are considered **hazardous**.
hot (adj)	/hɒt/	topaktuell	Find out what's **hot** and what's not in the music scene.
quarterly (adj)	/ˈkwɔːtəlɪ/	vierteljährlich erscheinend	A **quarterly** newsletter appears four times a year.
coverage (n)	/ˈkʌvərɪdʒ/	Bericht	Our website features complete **coverage** from our guidebooks.
dispatch (n)	/dɪˈspætʃ/	Bericht	Our online newsletter features **dispatches** from our authors on the road.
hotbed (n)	/ˈhɒtbed/	Brutstätte	According to the media, the shantytowns are **hotbeds** of crime and disease.
hypertext link (n)	/ˈhaɪpətekst ˌlɪŋk/	Hyperlink	Click on the **hypertext links** to find out more.
opening (n)	/ˈəʊpnɪŋ/	Möglichkeit	Visit our website to find out about new career **openings**.
policy (n)	/ˈpɒləsɪ/	Police	Click here to see the different types of insurance **policy** on offer.
shantytown (n)	/ˈʃæntɪˌtaʊn/	Armenviertel	Read about the **shantytowns** of South Africa on our website.
update (n)	/ˈʌpdeɪt/	Update, aktualisierte Information	Click on the 'News' hyperlink for **updates** on Rough Guide events.
check out (phr v)	/tʃek ˈaʊt/	sich anschauen	**Check out** our new range of CDs on our website.
lie behind (phr v)	/ˌlaɪ bɪˈhaɪnd/	dahinterstecken	What **lies behind** the popular image of Cape Town's shantytowns?
tune into (phr v)	/ˈtjuːn ɪn ˌtə/	einschalten	You can **tune into** live music broadcasts on the web.
enlighten (v)	/ɪnˈlaɪtn/	informieren	Our guides aim to entertain and **enlighten**.
exhibit (v)	/ɪgˈzɪbɪt/	ausstellen	We will be **exhibiting** at the Caribbean Travel Show.
redesign (v)	/ˌriːdɪˈzaɪn/	neu entwerfen	Think about how you would like to **redesign** the home page on p.129.
view (v)	/vjuː/	betrachten	**View** our catalogue online.

in aid of	/ɪn ˈeɪd əv/	zugunsten von	The Travel Show is being held **in aid of** Latin American charities.
in collaboration with	/ɪn kəˌlæbəˈreɪʃn wɪð/	in Zusammenarbeit mit	The Rough Guide CDs are produced **in collaboration with** World Music network.
on the road	/ˌɒn ðə ˈrəʊd/	reisend	We publish regular reports on our website from authors **on the road**.

Review (p.131–135)

fastest-selling (adj)	/ˈfɑːstəstˌselɪŋ/	am schnellsten verkauft	Harry Potter and the Goblet of Fire is the **fastest-selling** book in history.
navigational (adj)	/ˌnævɪˈgeɪʃənl/	Navigations-	Many of the planes and ships reported a failure of their **navigational** equipment.
revved up (adj)	/ˌrevd ˈʌp/	aufgedreht	Would you describe yourself as **revved up** or relaxed?
well documented (adj)	/ˌwel ˈdɒkjəmentəd/	gut dokumentiert	It is **well documented** that boys tend not to read books by female authors.
inexplicably (adv)	/ɪnɪkˈsplɪkəblɪ/	unerklärlicherweise	At the moment of his death all the lights in Cairo **inexplicably** went out.
abduction (n)	/əbˈdʌkʃn/	Entführung	Do you believe in alien **abduction**s?
bomber (n)	/ˈbɒmə(r)/	Bomber	The air force **bomber**s suddenly disappeared from radar.
curator (n)	/kjʊəˈreɪtə(r)/	Kurator	A **curator** is someone who is in charge of a museum.
curse (n)	/kɜːs/	Fluch	The **curse** of Tutankhamun was supposed to cause the death of anyone who disturbed his body.
patents office (n)	/ˈpeɪtənts ˌɒfɪs/	Patentamt	The **patents office** issues documents to people who have invented things to prevent other people from copying their idea.
release (n)	/rɪˈliːs/	Veröffentlichung	It sold 372,775 copies on the first day of its **release**.
remains (n pl)	/rɪˈmeɪnz/	Überreste	The **remains** of Tutankhamun were discovered on 26 November 1922.
training mission (n)	/ˈtreɪnɪŋ ˌmɪʃn/	Trainingsflug	The five bombers were out on a **training mission**.
date back to (phr v)	/deɪt ˈbæk tə/	datiert sein auf	The tradition **dates back to** medieval times.
go out (phr v)	/ˌgəʊ ˈaʊt/	ausgehen	All the lights in Cairo **went out** at the exact moment of his death.
howl (v)	/haʊl/	heulen	The dog began to **howl** and then died.
(be) at the planning stage	/(biː) ət ðə ˈplænɪŋ ˌsteɪdʒ/	im Planungsstadium	'Where are you going on holiday?' 'It**'s at the planning stage**.'
go with the flow	/ˌgəʊ wɪð ðə ˈfləʊ/	dem Strom folgen	Just relax and **go with the flow**.
leave nothing to chance	/liːv ˌnʌθɪŋ tə ˈtʃɑːns/	nichts dem Zufall überlassen	She's a a very organised person and **leaves nothing to chance**.
never to be seen again	/ˌnevə tə bɪ ˌsiːn əˈgen/	auf Nimmerwiedersehen	The bombers disappeared from radar **never to be seen again**.
(be) on the way down	/(biː) ɒn ðə ˌweɪ ˈdaʊn/	auf dem absteigenden Ast (sein)	Be nice to people when you're successful – you might meet them again **on the way down**.
(be) on the way out	/(biː) ɒn ðə ˌweɪ ˈaʊt/	außer Mode kommen	They reckoned guitar music **was on the way out**.
(be) on the way up	/(biː) ɒn ðə ˌweɪ ˈʌp/	auf dem Weg nach ober (sein)	It's important to be nice to people when you're **on the way up**.
be on top of things	/biː ɒn ˌtɒp əv ˈθɪŋz/	auf dem Laufenden sein	In a busy job like mine, it's important to **be on top of things**.
be open to offers	/biː ˌəʊpən tuː ˈɒfəz/	offen sein für Angebote	'What are you doing on Sunday?' '**I'm open to offers**.'
play truant	/pleɪ ˈtruːənt/	(die Schule) schwänzen	Parents were worried that children would **play truant** from school.
shortly after	/ˌʃɔːtlɪ ˈɑːftə(r)/	kurz nach	**Shortly after** this three of the archaeologists' assistants died.
the lot	/ðə ˈlɒt/	das Ganze	He ordered wine and scones and enjoyed **the lot** before finishing his exam.
four doors down	/ˌfɔː dɔːz ˈdaʊn/	4 Stockwerke unter	The name 'Potter' comes from a neighbour who lived **four doors down** from JK Rowling.
without trace	/wɪˌðaʊt ˈtreɪs/	spurlos	Planes and ships simply vanished **without trace**.

GRAMMAR REFERENCE

VERB STRUCTURES & AUXILIARY VERBS (Unit 1, p.8)

Verb structures

English combines present or past time with the simple, continuous or perfect aspect to form different tenses.

Present verb structures

You use the present simple mainly to talk about habits and routines or things that are always true.
*I usually **go** to bed around midnight.*
*Pictures **say** more than words.*

You can use the present continuous to talk about activities that are in progress now, or to describe changing situations.
*I**'m learning** Japanese as well as English.*
*The world's climate **is getting** warmer.*

Note that some verbs are not normally found in continuous forms. You will find more information about these verbs in unit 6.

You can use the present perfect to talk about present situations which started in the past and that are continuing now, or which exist because of a completed past event, or which happened at an indefinite time in the past.
*I**'ve been taking** English classes since last year.*
*Look, she**'s changed** her hairstyle.*
*We**'ve seen** Madonna in concert nine times!*

Past verb structures

You use the past simple to fix events and situations in the past.
*Nelson Mandela **was** in prison for twenty-seven years. He **was released** in 1990.*

You usually use the past continuous in contrast with the past simple to talk about activities that were in progress when something happened.
*He **was driving** to London when the accident **happened**.*

You use the past perfect to show clearly that one past event happened before another past event.
*The film **had started** when I arrived.*

You can use both *would* and *used to* to refer to regular or repeated past actions.
*When she was at school, she **used to** get up before six o'clock and **would** always have tea for breakfast.*

You can also use *used to* – but not *would* – to refer to past states or situations.
*I **used to** have a motorbike but I sold it a few years ago.*

Auxiliary verbs

The auxiliary verbs *be*, *have* and *do* are used to form different verb structures. They are also used with *so* and *neither/nor* in question tags and in short answers.

So & neither

You use *so* to mean 'also' in the structure *So + auxiliary + subject*.
*'I'm American.' '**So am I.**'*
*'I've been to New York.' '**So has my sister.**'*
*'He fell in love.' '**So did she.**'*

You use *neither* or *nor* to mean 'also not' in the same structure.
*'I don't like warm beer.' '**Neither do I.**'*
*'I didn't use to like biology.' '**Nor did I.**'*
*'I can't swim.' '**Neither can my brother.**'*

Both *so* and *neither* are used to show agreement between speakers. Note what happens when there is disagreement between speakers.
'I'm Irish.' 'I'm not.' (NOT ~~I'm not Irish.~~)
'He hasn't got a car.' 'She has.' (NOT ~~She's.~~)
'I didn't see the match.' 'We did.' (NOT ~~We'd.~~)

Question tags & short answers

You usually use a negative question tag with a positive statement, and a positive question tag with a negative statement.

+   -   -   +

You're Irish, aren't you? | You're not Irish, are you?
It's cold today, isn't it? | It isn't cold today, is it?

You use *they* to refer to *somebody, anybody, everybody* and *nobody*.
***Somebody** must have called earlier, mustn't **they**?*

You use a positive question tag after *never, hardly, little.*
*He **never** gives up, **does** he?*

You can use *will/would* or *can/can't/could* after imperatives.
***Get** me some milk from the shops, **would** you?*

Other cases:
Let's go out for dinner, **shall** we?
There's no time left, is **there**?
Nothing can go wrong, can **it**?
To answer *Yes/No* questions you can use the structure *Yes* or *No* + subject + auxiliary.
'Have you been working?' 'Yes, I have. / No, I haven't.'

INDIRECT QUESTIONS (Unit 1, p.12)

Indirect questions are often used when you want to be more polite or tentative, because, for example, you are starting a conversation with someone you don't know or you are asking a sensitive personal question. The word order is the same as in normal statements: subject + verb. In *Wh-* questions you use the same question word. In *Yes/No* questions you use *if* or *whether*.

Question frame		Subject	Verb
Do you mind telling me	what	the time	is, please?
Would you mind showing me	how	this	works, please?
Do you have any idea	when	they	are arriving?
I'd like to know	where	she	buys (her shoes).
Could you tell me	who	they	have invited?
I was wondering	if/whether	you	could help me.
What time	do you suppose	they	will get here?
What	does he think	he	is doing?

VERB PATTERNS (Unit 2, p.18)

Verbs followed by the *to*-infinitive

1   The following verbs don't typically take an object before the *to*-infinitive: *aim, arrange, attempt, can't afford, decide, hope, intend, manage, offer, plan, refuse, seem, tend, try.*
She **manages to stay** in shape.
We **tend to go** on camping holidays.

2   The following verbs *sometimes* take an object before the *to*-infinitive: *expect, help, pay, prefer, want, would like.*
I **wanted to go out** but I couldn't afford to.
I **wanted her to go out** with me, but she said she was busy.

3   The following verbs *usually* take an object before the *to*-infinitive: *allow, encourage, force, invite, order, remind, teach, urge, warned (not).*
My father **taught me to swim** when I was five.
My parents **allowed me to go** to the party.

Make & let

After *make* and *let* you use the infinitive without *to*.

She **makes me cuddle** her.
(NOT ... ~~makes me to cuddle~~)

They **let me have** my own beliefs.
(NOT ... ~~let me to have~~ ...)

Verbs followed by the *-ing* form

You use the *-ing* form after the following verbs: *avoid, can't stand, consider, detest, dislike, don't mind, dread, enjoy, fancy, finish, keep, miss, spend/waste time.*
My mother **keeps embarrassing** me.
I **can't stand being** the centre of attention.

You will find more about verbs followed by both the *to*-infinitive and the *-ing* form in unit 5.

Verb + preposition structures

You use the *-ing* form after verb + preposition structures: *accuse someone of, apologise for, approve of, believe in, blame someone for, concentrate on, congratulate someone on, consist of, dream about/of, forgive someone for, insist on, look forward to, object to, prevent someone from, rely on, specialise in, succeed in, think of, worry about.*
Gina's mother **succeeds in staying** slim.
I **look forward to hearing** from you.

ADJECTIVE STRUCTURES (Unit 2, p.21)

Adjective + *to*-infinitive

An adjective can be followed by a *to*-infinitive in the following structure.
It's **difficult to know** with Sarah.
The poor chap is **unlikely to last** very long.

Adjective + *for* + object + *to*-infinitive

If you need to mention a specific person or type of person, use *for* + object between the adjective and the *to*-infinitive.
*It's important **for him** to have some qualifications.*
*It's easy **for me** to hide at work.*
Note: You don't say: ~~For me~~ *it's easy to hide at work.*

Adjectives + dependent prepositions

Many adjectives are followed by a particular preposition. Here is a list of some of the more common ones.

certain about	optimistic about	serious about	good at	hopeless at	useless at
famous for	late for	ready for	covered in	interested in	lacking in	afraid of
fond of	proud of	dependent on	keen on	reliant on	accustomed to	allergic to
used to	angry with	compatible with	fed up with		

ARTICLES (Unit 3, p.28)

Articles can be difficult to use correctly: the rules are many and complex. Here are some of the most important rules.

No article

You don't use articles with proper nouns such as places, people and companies.
*There was a young lady from **Niger**.*
***John Smith** had a job with **Microsoft** but now he's moved to **IBM**.*
Exceptions are when the article is part of a name (***The United States, The BBC, The Beatles***).

The indefinite article means 'one', so you don't use it with plurals or uncountable nouns.
*There are plenty of **ideas**. The love of **money** is the root of all evil.*
Note: In English, most abstract concepts are uncountable: *After a few years of **hard work** ...*

Indefinite article: introducing/categorising

When you first mention new people, places or objects etc., the most normal thing to do is to *introduce* them by saying what *category* they belong to. You use the indefinite article to show that this is what you are doing.
*There was **a young lady** from Niger*
*Who smiled as she rode on **a tiger**.*

Definite article: referring/identifying

When you *identify* something or *refer* to a *specific* thing, you use the definite article. This often happens for one of these two reasons.

1 Back reference:
*They came back from **the ride***
*With **the lady** inside*
*And **the smile** on the face of **the tiger**.*
The last three lines of the poem refer to things introduced in the first two. We now know which specific lady, tiger, ride and smile the poet is referring to.

2 Shared knowledge:
*You could be calmly sitting on **the beach**, dozing in **the sun** and looking at **the ocean**.*
It's obvious which beach, sun and ocean the tourist is talking about.

Back reference and shared knowledge can combine.
*He took **a photograph**. **The click** of **the camera** woke the man up.*
We know that to take a photograph you need a camera, and that most cameras go click when you take a picture.

Note: In general statements in English you don't usually use the definite article with plural or uncountable nouns.
Men are a mystery to women. Time is money.

UNREAL CONDITIONALS (Unit 3, p.31)

Most conditional sentences have two clauses: the *if*-clause and the main clause.
1 The *if*-clause describes a condition: ***If I were rich, ...*** It usually starts with the conjunction, *if*. (You'll find further information on *if*-clauses in unit 9.)
2 The main clause comments on the condition in the *if*-clause: *... **I'd buy a yacht**.*
The two clauses can be used in either order: *I'd buy a yacht **if I were rich**.* In writing, when the *if*-clause comes first, use a comma to separate it from the main clause:
***If I were rich**, I'd buy a yacht.*

Types of conditional

Real conditionals are used to talk about real or possible events and situations.
If you see Max, can you give him this letter?
If it rained, we usually played indoors.

Unreal conditionals are used to talk about events and situations which are imaginary, untrue, impossible or unlikely.
If the world was flat, you would sail off the end.
If I were you, I'd give up smoking.

Backshifting

In the *if*-clause of an unreal conditional the tenses change. They *backshift*.

Backshift	Real situation	Unreal condition
present → past	I never **feel** I've got too much money ... We**'re not having** a party ... You **haven't done** your homework ...	If I ever **felt** ... If we **were having** ... If you**'d (had) done** ...
past → past perfect	I **didn't know** ...	If I**'d (had) known** ...

In the main clause you can use any of the four past modal auxiliaries: *would, could, should* or *might*. The most useful of these is *would*.

With any of the four auxiliaries, you can use the simple form (*would do*), the continuous (*would be doing*) or the perfect (*would have done*), as appropriate.
If I ever felt that I had too much money, **I'd give** some to charity.
If we were having a party, we**'d invite** you.
If you'd done your homework, you **wouldn't be having** these problems.
If I'd known they were valuable antiques, **I'd have kept** them.

The perfect form is used when the main clause refers to the past.

If + *was*/*were* in unreal conditionals

In spoken and written English, you will find both *If I **was*** and *If I **were*** (*rich*). Both are acceptable, though many people consider *were* to be more correct.

If	I you he/she/it we they	were	rich, ... famous, ... less busy, ... better organised, ... able to come, ...

Note: *Were* is always used in the expression *If I were you*, which is used to give advice.

SYMPATHY, ADVICE & RECOMMENDATIONS (Unit 4, p.36)

Showing sympathy

You can use any of the following expressions to sympathise with someone.
Poor you.
Oh dear.
That must be awful.
I know what you mean.

If you are not sympathetic you can use the following.
Serves you right.
You've only got yourself to blame.
If you hadn't ... you wouldn't be ... now.

Giving advice & making recommendations

There are lots of ways of giving advice or making recommendations. The expression you use will normally depend on the formality of the situation.

Typical in conversation:
Have you tried + noun / *-ing*?
You could try + noun / *-ing*
If I were you, I'd ...
If you ask me, you should / you need to ...
Imperatives

Typical in written or more formal situations:
It's important (not) to ...
It's best (not) to ...
It's a good idea to ...

PHRASAL VERBS (Unit 4, p.41)

The term 'phrasal verb' usually refers to all multi-word verbs, consisting of a verb + particle(s).

The meaning of phrasal verbs

Sometimes the meaning is obvious from the verb and the particle (*sit down, go away*). Other times just the particle may help you work out the meaning (*sum up, do up, clean up, drink up, use up,* etc. 'up' = completing/finishing).
Most of the time though you should approach phrasal verbs like you do any other new lexical item: learn the exact meaning, notice how the word is used in context and frequently revise your examples.

The grammar of phrasal verbs

Phrasal verbs can be divided into four basic grammatical types.

1 verb + particle

Some phrasal verbs are intransitive and so do not take a direct object.
*Without any more help, we just can't **go on**.*
*The plane **takes off** at 3.55 this afternoon.*

55

2 verb + object + particle (separable)

The biggest group of phrasal verbs are transitive. When the direct object is a noun, you can usually put it before or after the particle.
*She **picks** foreign languages **up** very quickly.*
*She **picks up** foreign languages very quickly.*

When the direct object is a pronoun, you must put it between the verb and the particle.
*I can honestly say that I've never **let** her **down**.* (NOT ~~let down her~~ ...)
*I can't hear. **Turn** it **up**, will you?* (NOT ~~Turn up it~~ ...)

3 verb + particle + object (not separable)

With this type of phrasal verb you always put the direct object - noun or pronoun - after the particle.
*It took him a long time to **get over** the divorce.*
*I don't think he ever wants to **go through** it again.*

4 verb + particle + particle + object (not separable)

Similar to type 3, you always put the direct object - noun or pronoun - after the second particle.
*I didn't **find out about** her boyfriend till after the party.*
*I don't know how she **puts up with** him.*

VERBS + *TO*-INFINITIVE & *-ING* FORM (Unit 5, p.45)

to-infinitive or *-ing* form?

Many verbs are followed either by the *to*-infinitive (*he managed to pay, they taught her to ski*, etc.) or by the *-ing* form (*she enjoys reading, I miss hearing her voice*, etc.). You will find more information about these verbs in unit 2.

There is a small group of verbs which can be followed by both the *to*-infinitive and the *-ing* form. The meaning can change significantly depending on which form is used.

1 remember, forget

With the *to*-infinitive you can talk about actions somebody is/was supposed to do.
*I **remembered to buy** her a birthday card.*
*But I **forgot to post** it.*

With the *-ing* form you refer to definite events - things that people actually did.
*I **remember** meeting her in a bar.* = I met her and now I remember this meeting.
*I'll **never forget kissing** her for the first time.* = I kissed her and I'll never forget the kiss.
Note: *forget* + *-ing* form is usually only used with *never*.

2 stop

With the *-ing* form you are saying that an activity has stopped.
*She **stopped talking** to him after that last argument.*

With the *to*-infinitive you are giving the reason for stopping.
*She **stopped to tell** me about her boyfriend when I saw her in town.*

3 try

With the *to*-infinitive you try something but can't do it.
*I **tried to make** her understand my feelings, but she wouldn't listen.* = I didn't manage to make her understand.

With the *-ing* form you try something to see what the outcome will be.
*I **tried leaving** her messages, but she never replied.* = I managed to leave messages, but they didn't work.

Note: You can use *try* + *-ing* form as an alternative to *try* + *to*-infinitive in most cases.

4 like, love, hate

With the *to*-infinitive, you can imply that you think something is a good (or bad) idea to do.
*I **like to do** my tax returns early.*

With the *-ing* form you state your real feelings about something.
*I **hate doing** my tax returns.*

Note: *like, love*, etc. + *to*-infinitive can also be used to state your real feelings about something.
would + *like/love/hate* etc. is always followed by the *to*-infinitive.
*I'd **love to visit** China.*

Note: *Help, go on, come* and other verbs can also be followed by the *to*-infinitive or the *-ing* form (with a change in meaning).

PRESENT AND PAST HABITS (Unit 5, p.49)

The most common way of speaking about habit is by using a simple tense with an adverb of frequency or adverb phrase.
*As a student, she **got up** late **every morning**.*
*She **hardly ever did** any work.*
*Now, she **always gets up at seven o'clock**.*

Will & would

If you want to emphasize that you are talking about actions (not states) which are characteristic and predictable, you can use *will* or *won't* for the present and *would* (*'d*) for the past.

He**'ll get up** at seven o'clock every morning.
He **won't talk** to anyone until he's finished his breakfast.
I**'d walk** to school every day unless it was raining, when my mum**'d take** me.

Will and *would* are almost always contracted (*'ll*, *'d*). If you use the full forms, it can make you sound angry. (See *Annoying habits*.)

Used to

You can use this structure to talk about past habits or past states or situations.
I **used to come** home every day at five o'clock.
I **didn't use to enjoy** sports lessons.

Annoying habits

You can use *will* to show annoyance about the way somebody behaves, especially with *insist on* + *-ing* form and *keep* + *-ing* form. In this case, *will* is almost never contracted.
She **will insist on opening** all the windows.

You can also use *always/forever* + continuous to produce the same effect.
She**'s always telling** me what to do.
He **was always asking** people embarrassing questions.

Note: This structure is not always negative.
I loved Sara. She **was always making** jokes.

DYNAMIC & STATIVE MEANINGS (Unit 6, p.55)

Dynamic meanings

Most verbs have dynamic meanings. They describe either single acts (*hit*, *knock*, *throw*) or activities and processes (*change*, *eat*, *walk*, *work*). Something 'happens'.
Someone**'s knocking** at the door. (repeated acts)
I**'ve been working** here all my life. (continuous activity)
The world's climate **has become** warmer. (process)

Stative meanings

Verbs with stative meanings usually describe a state of mind (verbs connected with knowledge, emotion or perception) or a state of affairs (verbs connected with being or having). Nothing 'happens'.
I**'ve known** my best friend for more than ten years.
She **has** two laptops and a huge desktop machine.
I can't **see** a thing without my glasses.

Note: The continuous form has a dynamic meaning, and so you cannot normally use verbs with stative meanings in the continuous form.
~~I've been knowing my best friend for more than ten years.~~
Verbs with stative meanings are also normally not used in the imperative form.

Dynamic & stative meanings

Some verbs can have both dynamic and stative meanings.

Dynamic	Stative
I**'ve been having** driving lessons recently. (= taking)	I **have** an old yellow bicycle. (= possess)
I**'m seeing** the dentist this afternoon. (= visiting)	Do you **see** what I mean? (= understand)

PRESENT PERFECT SIMPLE & CONTINUOUS (Unit 6, p.58)

The present perfect shows a connection between the past and the present. Whether you use the simple or continuous forms will often depend on whether the verb has a dynamic meaning or a stative meaning.

Verb with dynamic meaning + present perfect continuous

This combination can express actions, activities or processes which are incomplete or ongoing. They started in the past and continue now.
I**'ve been doing** this job since I was 21.
How long **have you been saving** with the same bank?

Note: Although generally the present perfect continuous is preferred for incomplete actions, activities or processes, occasionally you may want to emphasise the permanence of the action, activity or process. In these circumstances you can use the present perfect simple. Compare:
I**'ve lived / worked** in the same town all my life. (permanent, state-like situation)
I**'ve been living / working** in Paris for the last few months. (temporary, dynamic)

Verb with dynamic meaning + present perfect simple

This combination can express actions, activities or processes which are completed. They have 'happened' in a period of time up to and including the present.
*He's **tried** to climb Everest **three times**.*
*I've **only missed** a plane **once in my life**.*

Verb with stative meaning + present perfect simple

This combination can express a situation which is incomplete or ongoing. It started in the past and continues now.
*I've **had** my trusty old Land Rover for years.*
*How long **have you known** your English teacher?*

Note: You cannot normally use verbs with stative meanings in the present perfect continuous.

REPORTING VERBS (Unit 8, p.72)

When you use reporting verbs such as *advise* and *explain*, it's important to know if the hearer is the direct object.

1   With verbs like *tell* the hearer is the direct object.

*Mrs Pattinson advised **him** / invited **them** / reminded **us***	*to vote for her.*
*She convinced **us** / persuaded **me** / reassured **everyone***	*that she was telling the truth.*
*He accused **me** of / informed **them** about / congratulated **her** on*	*giving up.*

2   With verbs like *say* where the hearer is NOT the direct object.

Mrs Pattinson explained / announced / suggested	*that we should vote for her.*
She agreed / refused / proposed	*to tell the truth.*
He admitted / insisted on / denied	*giving up.*

If you want to mention the hearer with the following common reporting verbs, *admit, announce, complain, explain, mention, propose, say, suggest*, you can use *to* + hearer and then a *that* clause.
*She complained **to the engineer** that her computer kept crashing.*
*He explained **to the class** that he would be away for a few days.*
*I suggested **to Don and Liz** that we all went on holiday together.*

PASSIVE STRUCTURES (Unit 9, p.82)

Passive report structures

These structures can be used to say what people in general feel or believe.
You can find them in formal contexts such as scientific writing or in news reports.

	is	said
It	has been	believed that ...
	was	thought

*It **used to be said that** beauty was in the eye of the beholder.*

He/She/It	is/was	said	
They	are/were	believed	to (+ infinitive) ...
		thought	

*But now beauty **is thought to be** objective and quantifiable.*

Other verbs that can be used in this way include: *alleged, assumed, claimed, considered, expected, felt, reckoned, regarded, reported, rumoured, suggested.*

Have/Get something done

You can use this structure when someone does something for you - often because you have paid them to do it.

have/get + something (object) + past participle

*I'll probably **have/get my car repaired** next week.*
*How many times has she **had/got her fortune told**?*
*You really should **have/get your eyes tested**.*

Note: *Get* is a little less formal than *have*.

UNREAL CONDITIONAL CLAUSES - ALTERNATIVES TO *IF* (Unit 9, p.86)

You usually begin an unreal conditional clause with *if*, but when you are making questions, there are various other alternatives.

Conditional clause

If		past simple
Imagine (that)		past continuous
Supposing (that)	subject	*were to* + infinitive
Suppose (that)		*might*
Assuming (that)		past perfect

Main clause

(question word)	would could might	subject	infinitive be + present participle ? have + past participle

Imagine you **were meeting** someone for the first time, how **would** you **introduce** yourself?
Suppose you **didn't enjoy** the first date, **would** you still **go** on a second date?
Assuming that you **were to go** on another date, where **might** you **be planning** to meet?
Supposing that neither of the dates **had been** successful, what **might** you **tell** the person?

MODALS OF DEDUCTION (Unit 10, p.93)

When we want to speculate or make deductions about a particular situation, we can use the following modal verbs:
*   *must*, *can't* when we are 99% sure about something.
*   *may (not)*, *might (not)*, *could* when we think something is possible.

These modal verbs can be followed by present and past infinitives.
Present: *It can't **be** as bad as all that!*
         *I think he might **be working** late today.*
Past: *Diego may **have found out** about Frida's affair.*
         *Sorry, I must **have been daydreaming**.*

NARRATIVE TENSE STRUCTURES (Unit 10, p.96)

Past simple

The past simple is usually used to fix events in the past. You can use it to describe the main events of a story.
*Trevor Baylis **dozed off** and **had** a dream.*

Past continuous

The past continuous is often used in contrast with the past simple. You can use it to describe an activity which was in progress when the main events of the story happened.
*Art Fry **was listening** to the sermon one Sunday when his mind began to wander.*

Past perfect simple & continuous

The past perfect can be used to refer to an event (simple) or activity in progress (continuous) which clearly took place before the time of the main events of the story.
*Epperson discovered his glass of lemonade still sitting where he **had left** it.*

RELATIVE CLAUSES (Unit 11, p.103)

Relative clauses are usually found after a noun or a noun phrase. Like adjectives, they describe or give information about the person or thing being talked or written about.

Non-defining relative clauses

You use non-defining relative clauses to give extra, non-essential information about the person or thing you are talking about. You can also comment on the whole of the main clause. You always begin a non-defining relative clause with a relative pronoun, and you separate it from the main clause with commas.

*He's going out with Julie, **who** I can't stand.* (extra information about Julie)
*He's going out with Julie, **which** I can't stand.* (comment on the whole of the main clause)
*He's going out with Julie, **whose** brother is my boss.* (extra information about Julie)

Pronouns for non-defining relative clauses:

	Person	Thing
Subject	... , who ...	... , which ...
Object	... , who (whom) ...	... , which ...
Possessive	... , whose ...	... , whose ...

Defining relative clauses

You use defining relative clauses to state exactly which person or thing you are talking about. When the relative pronoun is the subject of the relative clause you must use *who*, *that* or *which*.
*I like friends **who** never let me down.*
*I want a bank account **that** never runs out.*

When the relative pronoun is the object of the relative clause you can omit *who*, *that* or *which*.
*He's got a job (**that/which**) he's really interested in.*
*She's got a boyfriend (**who**) she's really in love with.*

You can never omit *whose*.
*That's the man **whose** dog bit my son.*
*John's the boy **whose** mum I met last week.*

When the relative pronoun is the object of the relative clause, you don't need another object pronoun.
She got a new car that she's very proud of. (NOT ... proud of ~~it~~.)
He's the man whose case I took by mistake. (NOT ... whose case I took ~~it~~.)

Pronouns for defining relative clauses:

	Person	Thing
Subject	... who / that ...	... that / which ...
Object	... (that / who) ...	... (that / which) ...
Possessive	... whose ...	... whose ...

EMPHASIS (CLEFT SENTENCES) (Unit 11, p.106)

What structures (= *The thing(s) that*)

You can use *What ... is/was ...* to emphasise either the subject or the object of a sentence.
Classical music *often helps me to concentrate.*
= *What often helps me to concentrate is **classical music**.*
*I don't understand **where they get this stuff from**.*
= *What I don't understand is **where they get this stuff from**.*

It is/was ... + relative clause

You can use this structure to emphasise almost any part of a sentence.
Brad Pitt married Jennifer Aniston in Los Angeles in 2000.
It was Brad Pitt *who married ...*
It was Jennifer Aniston *who married ...*
It was Los Angeles *where Brad Pitt married ...*
It was in 2000 *that Brad Pitt married ...*
You often use this structure when you are correcting what other people say.
It wasn't Gwyneth Paltrow *who married Brad Pitt. It was Jennifer Aniston.*

FUTURE FORMS (Unit 12, p.114)

Will ('ll), *(be) going to*, present continuous

These are the three most common forms for talking about the future.

1   *Will ('ll)* - predictions/decisions reacting to circumstances such as offers, promises and requests.
    *It'**ll** be worth a fortune in a few years' time.*
    *I'**ll** give you my photograph now if you like.*

2   *(be) going to* - intentions/predictions based on present evidence.
    *I'**m going to** concentrate on my musical career.*
    *Look at those clouds. It'**s going to** pour down.*

3   The present continuous - plans/arrangements
    *I'**m moving** to London next month.*

Present simple

You can use this form to talk about fixed future events: timetables, routines, schedules.
*My A-levels **start** next week.*
*The plane **leaves** at 15:40.*

Might & may

If you want to speculate about a future possibility you can use *might* or *may*.
*We **might** have to get a part-time job.*

Future continuous

You use this tense to talk about something happening around a certain time in the future.
*In five years' time I'**ll be staying** in posh hotels.*
*This time next week I'**ll be trekking** in Nepal.*

Future perfect

You use the future perfect to talk about something completed by a certain time in the future.
*By this time next year, we'**ll have had** a record in the charts.*
*The builder **will have finished** the kitchen walls by the end of the week.*

Verb structures after *if, when, as soon as ...*

When it is clear from the main clause that the sentence is about the future you don't use a future form in the subordinate clause.
When I leave school, I'm going to concentrate on my musical career.
(NOT ~~When I will leave school,~~ ...)
It'll be a miracle if she's passed the exam.
(NOT ... ~~if she will have passed the exam.~~)

Other conjunctions which introduce subordinate clauses: *after, as soon as, before, once, the moment, the minute, unless, until.*

60

QUANTITY (Unit 13, p.123)

You use determiners (*every*, *most*, *no*) and quantifiers (*all of*, *most of*, *none of*) to express quantity.

Which quantity expression?

1   The quantity expression you use depends on whether the noun is countable (C) or uncountable (U).
    *There's **far too much** stuff (U) in the room.*
    ***Not many of** the people (C) I work with smoke.*

    Sometimes you can use the same quantity expression for both countable and uncountable nouns.
    *He's got **loads of** money (U).*
    *I've got **loads of** coins (C) in my pocket.*

2   When there is an article (*a*, *an*, *the*), a possessive pronoun (*my*, *your*, etc.) or a demonstrative pronoun (*that*, *these*, etc.) before the noun, you use a quantity expression with *of*.
    *Several **of my** friends live in small villages.* (NOT ~~Several my friends~~ ...)
    *Most **of the** people in my neighbourhood go to work by car.* (NOT ~~Most of people~~ ...)

3   When you want to talk about small numbers or amounts you can use *a few* / *a little* to stress the positive (*some*) or *few* / *little* to stress the negative (*not many* / *much*).
    *We did it because we wanted to have **a little** fun.*
    *Please hurry up! There's very **little** time.*

Which verb form?

You use a singular verb form if the noun after *of* is uncountable or singular. You use a plural if the noun is countable.
*There**'s** lots of traffic (U) in the centre.*
*There **are** lots of tourists (C) in summer.*

THE PASSIVE (Unit 13, p.128)

There are several specific cases where you should use the passive.

1   When you don't know who the agent is. *The wheel **was invented** about 3,500 years ago.*
2   When the agent is obvious to everybody. *She **has been arrested** and **charged** with theft.*
3   When you don't want to identify the agent. *I **was told** not to mention it.*

The agent

If it is necessary to mention the agent of the passive (i.e. the 'doer' of the action), you use the preposition *by*. *Power will be provided **by a hundred engines at the rear**.*

ALPHABETICAL INDEX

attic conversion (n) p.21
availability (n) p.39
award-winning (adj) p.50

B

baby-faced (adj) p.29
back on to (phr v) p.28
backer (n) p.36
background (n) p.6
backpacking (n) p.45
backroads (n pl) p.7
backside (n) (TS) p.36
bagful (n) p.28
balanced diet (n) p.13
ball girl (n) p.4
ban (v) p.11
band together (phr v) p.9
bang (v) p.18
banisters (n) p.47
barbed wire (n) p.49
bash (v) p.45
basis (n) p.14
be after sb p.31
be all over sb like a rash (TS) p.32
be allergic to (adj) p.6
be at the end of one's tether p.45
be attracted to p.7
be best suited to p.44
be bound to p.28
be confined to p.35
be crammed with (adj) p.37
be dying for (TS) p.15
be embodied in p.30
be greeted with p.50
be hooked up to sth p.23
be in pain p.45
be in the way p.9

be in touch (with) p.7
be influenced by (TS) p.30
be intent on p.9
be involved with p.3
be mistaken for p.28
be more concerned with p.43
be on (one's) last legs p.46
be on one's way to p.15
be on top of things p.51
be one of the lads p.17
be open to offer p.51
be out and about p.31
be registered in sb's name p.26
be required to (TS) p.39
be starving p.12
be stirred to do sth (TS) p.36
be swarming with p.46
be tempted to do sth (TS) p.11
be the mistress of p.3
be the type to do sth p.27
be under fire (TS) p.41
be unlikely to p.7
be up to one's eyes in p.7
be up to sth p.18
be worth a fortune p.11
be worth one's while p.10
bearing in mind (that) p.13
beauty is in the eye of the p.30
become aware of p.3
become clear p.16
bedroom culture (n) p.22
bedside table (n) p.11
beg (v) (TS) p.41
behave oneself (v) p.11
benefit (v) (TS) p.9
best man (n) p.19
best-selling (adj) p.14

beyond the reach of p.25
biggest-selling (adj) p.20
big-headed (adj) (TS) p.32
birth-rate (n) p.43
bite off (phr v) p.17
black out (phr v) p.45
blade (n) p.45
blame (v) p.3
blanket (n) p.18
bleary-eyed (adj) p.48
blind date (n) p.31
blinds (n pl) p.47
bliss (n) (TS) p.26
bloke (n) p.15
blow kisses p.18
blow out (phr v) (TS) p.40
blow sth on sth (phr v) p.11
blow up (phr v) p.45
boarding school (n) p.43
bob (n) p.2
body language (n) (TS) p.32
boiling (adj) p.17
bolt (n) p.47
bomber (n) p.51
bone structure (n) p.29
bookish (adj) p.27
book-lover (n) p.22
bookmark (n) p.37
bored stiff p.42
bounce into (phr v) p.2
bra top (n) p.2
brainchild (n) p.34
brainwash (v) p.38
brand (n) p.38
brand awareness (n) p.39
brand loyalty (n) p.38
breadwinner (n) p.11

68

Macmillan Education
Between Towns Road, Oxford, OX4 3PP, UK
A division of Macmillan Publishers Limited
Companies and representatives throughout the world

ISBN 1 405 02831 9

Text, design and illustration © Macmillan Publishers Limited 2003

First published 2003

Original design spec by Rani Rai-Quantrill. Designed by Red Giraffe

Printed in Spain by Edelvives.

2007 2006 2005 2004 2003
10 9 8 7 6 5 4 3 2 1